KEEPING & BREEDING
BUTTERFLIES
AND OTHER EXOTICA

KEEPING & BREEDING
BUTTERFLIES
AND OTHER EXOTICA

PRAYING MANTIS, SCORPIONS, STICK INSECTS, LEAF INSECTS LOCUSTS, LARGE SPIDERS AND LEAF-CUTTER ANTS

JOHN L. S. STONE

BLANDFORD

A BLANDFORD BOOK

First published in the UK 1992
by Blandford
(a Cassell imprint)
Villiers House
41/47 Strand
LONDON
WC2N 5JE

Distributed in the United States
by Sterling Publishing Co., Inc.
387 Park Avenue South, New York, NY 10016-8810

Distributed in Australia
by Capricorn Link (Australia) Pty Ltd
P.O. Box 665, Lane Cove, NSW 2066

British Library Cataloguing in Publication Data

**A catalogue record for this book is available
from the British Library**

ISBN 0-7137-2293-2

Typeset by Litho Link Ltd, Welshpool, Powys
Printed and bound by Biddles Ltd, Guildford and
King's Lynn

CONTENTS

*With love to my wife
Julie*

ACKNOWLEDGMENTS

The author would like to offer his grateful thanks to the following for their help in the production of this book:

To Dr David J. Stradling for all the knowledge he has given to me over the years pertaining to leaf-cutting ants.

To Professor N. A. Webber of the USA for extracts from one of his early university papers on leaf-cutting ants.

To my wife Julie for putting up with all the work involved in the production of this book, also for producing the excellent line drawings.

To Mr K. J. Packer, FRES, for much hard work in checking for technical errors.

To Mr Bob Fredrick for giving me many of the slides reproduced herein. The remainder of the slides are by the author.

To Mr Claude Rivers, FRES, for all the help he has given me over the years and for his discovery of the clever use of formaldehyde to sterilize butterfly eggs.

To Mr Steve A. Mason for his help over the years and for a special snip of information pertaining to the breeding of Hairstreak butterflies.

To Mrs Doreen Burdon for her splendid work on the production of the manuscript.

INTRODUCTION

Even as a child, I was fascinated by insects. When I was three, my mother used to take me to play in a park which had a huge duck pond surrounded by trees. I used to feed the ducks and make vain attempts to capture the dragonflies which darted across the water's edge in the summer.

My interest in insects was increased when, on my eighth birthday, I was given a book which I treasure to this day. Entitled *The Outdoor World, or Young Collector's Handbook* by W. Furneaux, FRGS, it was an old volume, having first been printed in 1894, but between those worn covers was a wealth of information: hundreds of good illustrations, some in colour, of butterflies and moths, plants, all kinds of insects, birds and their eggs, small animals, crustaceans, even fish and other pond life. Now I could identify many of the creatures I encountered, and found they took on a whole new meaning.

My parents died when I was still young, and my sister and I went to live with our aunt and uncle who later adopted us. Soon afterwards we all moved to a new house, and created a beautiful garden out of what was formerly a wilderness. We planted Golden Rod, Michaelmas Daisies, Sedum, Buddleia, Sweet William and Nasturtium; soon the garden was alive with insects, and my interest in them grew daily. I spent hours thumbing through my book, searching, identifying and learning.

The book also described in detail how to start a butterfly collection, and I decided to have a go. My first butterfly net

9

was made from an old silk stocking with a knot tied in the middle. With it I managed to capture a Large White and a Peacock. Meticulously following the book's ancient method, I set them out to dry. Next morning, I dashed out to inspect my handiwork, and found to my horror that one butterfly had been half eaten. Even as I stared in disbelief at my mutilated specimen, the culprit arrived for another helping: it was a wasp. Before I could find a suitable weapon, the criminal settled on my precious butterfly and, with deft precision, snipped off the remaining wings with powerful mandibles. My vengeful thoughts now forgotten, I observed the demolition of my second butterfly with rapt attention, making new discoveries through the loss of my small collection.

Shortly afterwards, I captured a Garden Tiger moth, and was delighted when it laid some eggs in its jar. Soon I was the proud owner of several ravenous caterpillars, which in turn developed into ebony black chrysalids. I was never to see the adults emerge, however, thanks to some well-meaning relations who were staying with my step-parents; my anger at discovering that my chrysalids had been washed down the drain remains a vivid and painful memory.

About a year later, we moved to the Cotswolds. For a boy like myself, with a passionate interest in wildlife, this was absolute heaven. It was here that I first glimpsed the blue butterflies. For me, there was something magical about blue in a butterfly, and I used to spend all my days in the summer meadows, reluctant to go indoors even for meals.

In later years, I bred several species of butterflies, including Small Tortoiseshells, Peacocks, Large Whites, and my then favourite Common Blue; I also had limited success with the Small Copper. In addition to breeding butterflies, I kept as pets an owl, a jackdaw, a stock dove, a wild rabbit, field voles, lizards, and several grass snakes. I reared frogs and toads, which I watched as they developed from egg to adult, and newts. I enjoyed seeing the newts lay their eggs, wrapping a leaf around each one with their tiny hand-like rear feet.

Introduction

I find it difficult to express how grateful and privileged I feel for having this almost fanatical interest in nature at so early an age. The fascination which I still feel for butterflies, and indeed all forms of wildlife, was inspired by the innocent wonder and admiration I had for the natural world around me. With the help of this book, I hope to share a little of my love for butterflies with you, the reader. Even if you are a complete novice, do have a go at breeding them, and discover how rewarding it can be. If you have children, why not encourage them to use the simple instructions in the following pages and breed some of our winged beauties? Remember, there is no substitute for the wonder of nature seen through the eyes of a child.

J.L.S.S.

PREFACE

Some species of insects are easy to breed, others are more difficult. The object of this book is to teach the basics of the breeding of various species, but with the emphasis on butterflies.

In 1971, in partnership with my friend John Midwinter, we set up the first exhibition of free-flying and breeding butterflies in the world at Bourton-on-the-Water, in Gloucestershire, England. From that small exhibit the idea of the larger walk-through butterfly farm came about, the first of which was opened a few years later in the Channel Islands.

Today there are about 70 such exhibitions in the United Kingdom and others are popping up all over the world; they are now big business.

When John Midwinter and I started the first one, we didn't dream where it would lead, and though most of the butterfly farms are primarily commercial ventures, one thing they all do is create a wider interest in nature's most beautiful of insects; they also make it easier for the amateur to obtain many species to try and breed.

Before the reader can set up the various methods described later in the book one has to learn more about the species; details such as when they fly, when they lay their eggs and on what foodplants the caterpillars feed.

The first part of this book deals with the life histories of about 80 species, mainly from the northern hemisphere from which most will be drawn from the wild. The more exotic species will mostly have to be purchased from dealers.

Butterflies and moths belong to the order Lepidoptera, or scaled winged insects, which takes in about 100,000 species. Of these, only about 10 per cent are butterflies.

Until quite recently any insect book would state that there are about three-quarters of a million species of insects worldwide and probably about the same number yet to be discovered. However, in the late 1980s two surveys carried out in rainforests of Papua New Guinea and South America are causing the scientists to think again. The latest thoughts are that worldwide there are probably 30 million species, most of which will become extinct before they have even been discovered, due to the destruction of the world's rainforests and other habitats.

Many of the world's most beautiful species of butterflies live in rainforests; when they are gone the earth will be a poorer place for their passing.

1. BUTTERFLIES OF TEMPERATE REGIONS

All of the butterflies described in the first section of this book are found in the British Isles. They occur in other regions as well, but their life histories described here relate to their British origin; consequently, egg-laying and flying times will vary in other parts of the world, and even their foodplants could be different.

HESPERIIDAE: Skippers

The Skippers derive their popular name from their frenzied, darting flight, which resembles that of a moth rather than a butterfly. They are very distinctive, and also the most primitive of the butterflies, being so closely linked with moths that some authorities have given them a separate status between the two.

One of the definitive characteristics of a moth is a bristle-and-catch device that couples the wings together. The Australian Skipper, *Euschemon rafflesia*, poses an awkward problem: the male of the species has the bristle-and-catch device, but the female does not, thus illustrating the unique position of this family, midway between the moths and butterflies. To be scientifically accurate, only the female can be said to be a true butterfly.

Skippers have short, powerful bodies and large, broad heads with prominent 'eyebrows'. The antennae are widely spaced, some heavily clubbed like the Cinnabar moth, and others hooked and pointed at their tips.

They enjoy basking in the sunshine on flower heads or dead grasses and, with two exceptions mentioned below, they settle in a most unusual resting position; the hindwings are held flat, and the forewings half closed at an angle of 45°. The narrow forewings are also held back at an acute angle, giving the butterfly a snub-nosed appearance.

The caterpillars construct shelters amongst the grasses on which they feed, and pupate inside flimsy cocoons; many rest loose, concealed in their shelters, others pupate succincti: attached to a stem by the cremaster (the end of the chrysalis) fixed to a pad of silk, and supported by a silken girdle.

Hesperiidae are a large family, widely distributed throughout the world, with the South American countries being the most densely populated. There are only eight British species, and these are divided into two subfamilies.

The Dingy Skipper and the Grizzled Skipper belong to the subfamily Pyrginae, and rest with their wings flat. The remaining British Skippers belong to the subfamily Hesperiinae, and rest in the strange manner described above.

Chequered Skipper
Carterocephalus palaemon Pallas

DISTRIBUTION: North Europe, across central and northern Asia to Japan, North America (Canada, Alaska, south to Minnesota, Wyoming, central California).

FOODPLANTS: Wood False Brome Grass (*Brachypodium sylvaticum*) is one of many grasses this species will take.

GENERAL NOTES
The Chequered Skipper has declined rapidly in Britain over the last few decades, and is now confined to one or two Scottish locations. It has never been a very common species, but used to occur in abundant localized colonies in several parts of England north of the Midlands. It is primarily a woodland species, frequenting woodland rides and clearings, as well as sheltered, uncultivated banks and hillsides.

Like most of the Skippers, this is a single-brooded species, first seen on the wing towards the end of May and throughout June. Its chequered wings make it distinct from any other Skipper, and there is little difference between male and female. However, the female is a little fatter-bodied, and the spotting is slightly paler.

When not feeding, these butterflies spend long periods settled amongst the grasses, in the summer sunshine.

Creamy-coloured eggs are laid in June on the foodplant, and hatch after about two weeks. The caterpillars are straw-coloured with pale brown stripes, and feed until the autumn between blades of grass drawn together with silk. Hidden in this way, the larva is virtually invisible, and overwinters in the same position in its final instar (period between each skin change). In the spring, the larva feeds up to full growth, and pupates in May, girdled on a grass stem.

The pupae of Skippers are well camouflaged and usually green, but those of the Chequered Skipper are straw-coloured with narrow reddish brown stripes, close together, running lengthwise from the thorax to the pointed tail-tip. The pupation site is normally close to the ground on a dead stem.

Large Skipper

Ochlodes venata Bremer and Grey

DISTRIBUTION: Europe, temperate Asia to China and Japan.

FOODPLANTS: Cocksfoot (*Dactylis glomerata*) is probably the principal foodplant, but others are also taken. Captive-bred larvae will accept many species of the coarser grasses.

GENERAL NOTES

This is the largest and most common of the British Skippers, being very well distributed in England as far north as Yorkshire, and also in Wales. Sunlit grassy hillsides and open wasteland are favourite haunts, and for this reason it is often found in the company of other grassland species, including the Common Blue, Brown Argus and other Skippers. If disturbed, the Large Skipper will fly up from underfoot to settle only a short distance away; when freshly emerged, its orange coloration is brilliant.

Thistle heads are often adorned with these butterflies, as they feed and rest on them for long periods, and once they find a patch of territory to their liking, they will chase off other butterflies that venture near.

The female lays her eggs on the stems and blades of coarse grasses, and these hatch after about two weeks. The larva draws the edges of a grass blade together with a considerable amount of silk to form a tube, and uses this shelter when not feeding, and also for hibernation.

The caterpillar is green, with a pale green stripe down each side. When ready to pupate, it constructs an almost moth-like cocoon, producing large amounts of multi-stranded silk to draw several blades of grass around itself. Inside the cocoon, the blackish chrysalis is loose, and has evolved the unusual feature of a separate proboscis case which extends to the tip of the abdomen.

Small Skipper
Thymelicus sylvestris Poda

DISTRIBUTION: Europe, north Africa, Asia Minor to Iran.

FOODPLANTS: Most species of soft grasses.

GENERAL NOTES

The Small Skipper is a very common species, well distributed in England and Wales, and found as far north as Lancashire and Yorkshire. Disused quarries, especially if damp and containing well-established, patchy vegetation, are ideal habitats for this butterfly. It is also attracted to scrubland, wasteland and rough, sheltered hillsides, where it will feed from thistles and other flowers. It will spend long periods settled amongst the grasses, or on sunlit flower heads, and if disturbed will depart rapidly with its moth-like flight.

These butterflies have a bright orange coloration. Males can be easily distinguished by a black line of scent scales running from the centre of the forewing to the hind margin close to the thorax.

The Small Skipper, *T. sylvestris*, is difficult to distinguish from the Essex Skipper, *T. lineola* (see below). Only close examination reveals that the antennae of *T. sylvestris* are bright orange underneath, while those of *T. lineola* have black tips on the underside. The Small Skipper is much more widespread than the Essex Skipper, even in the Thames Estuary, where Essex Skipper is quite common.

The Small Skipper is a single-brooded species, emerging in late June, and is on the wing until early September. Eggs are laid in small groups on the foodplant soon after the butterflies appear, and the larvae go straight into hibernation, often eating their eggshells and spinning tiny silken cocoons in which they overwinter.

In April the caterpillars commence feeding on tender spring growth in the grasses, progressing through five instars. They are green in colour with creamy green stripes down each side, and they pupate towards the end of June. The chrysalis is fixed by the cremaster and girdled in an upright position, usually on a grass stem, but before pupation the caterpillar pulls several blades of grass around its main stem, and these are held in place by strands of silk. Camouflage of the pupa is exceptionally good: the wing cases are a little darker in colour than the main pupal shell, but the overall colour is green, and it is therefore completely lost amongst the webbed grasses.

Essex Skipper

Thymelicus lineola Ochsenheimar

DISTRIBUTION: Europe, north Africa, northern Asia, North America (Minnesota, New Jersey, south to Maryland and Illinois).

FOODPLANTS: This species favours the coarser grasses, but will also take False Brome Grass (*Brachypodium*) and Couch Grass (*Elymus repens*).

GENERAL NOTES
The Essex Skipper is much more localized than the Small Skipper in England, being confined to the south-eastern counties with a few colonies in central southern England. It will often share its habitat with the Small Skipper and the Common Blue, inhabiting marginal woodlands, rough grassy banks and old quarries.

As in the Small Skipper (see above), the male has a black line of scent scales running from the centre of the forewing, but this line tends to be shorter, less oblique, and running straight to the base of the wing rather than to the hind margin. The black tip to the underside of the antenna is the only certain way of distinguishing this species from the Small Skipper, which it closely resembles in appearance and behaviour.

The eggs are laid in rows inside the sheath of a grass stem. The larvae form inside the shells, and then lie dormant until the following spring. In early June, the eggs hatch and the caterpillars begin to feed on the tender spring grasses. The larvae are slightly longer and more slender than those of *T. sylvestris*, and during the final instar their bodies have a slight blue tinge. When ready to pupate, the larva constructs a tent by drawing several blades of grass together with silk, and, thus concealed, the chrysalis is formed, held by the tail and girdled in an upright position to a grass stem. The adults emerge in July after about 15 days, some two weeks later than the Small Skipper.

Lulworth Skipper

Thymelicus acteon Rottemburg

DISTRIBUTION: Canary Isles, north Africa, southern and central Europe to Asia Minor.

FOODPLANTS: Chalk False Brome Grass (*Brachypodium pinnatum*) is the usual reported foodplant, but the larvae eat many others in the wild. Captive larvae have been reared on many species of grasses.

GENERAL NOTES
The Lulworth Skipper is a very localized species in Britain, being distributed only in the coastal areas of Dorset and south Devon. However, within these confines it is common. The butterflies frequent cliffs and open terrain, feeding from wild flowers, such as thistles and restharrow (*Ononis repens*).

The Lulworth Skipper is on the wing from early July until the end of August. It is much duller in colour than the other orange species of Skipper, and the sexes are easily distinguished. The male is slightly smaller than the female, and, though quite dark in colour, the characteristic scent scales running as a black streak from the wing to the thorax are still visible.

On the forewings of the female are about seven pale orange elongated spots forming a curved pattern across the wing from the leading edge. This pattern can also be found, although slightly less distinct, on the underside, and is completely absent from the male. Eggs are laid in rows of about 12. After hatching, the tiny larvae first eat the eggshells, and then spin small white cocoons inside which they immediately hibernate. In the spring, the caterpillars remain in small groups, constructing tube-like shelters inside blades of grass, and from these they feed up to full growth through five instars. The larval stage occupies about 10 months of the insect's life. The caterpillar is very similar to that of the Essex Skipper, but a paler green.

When fully grown, the larva draws a few blades of grass together with silk, and pupates in the girdled position, upright on a grass stem. The pupa is pale green, surrounded by wisps of silken thread. One brood is produced each season.

Silver-spotted Skipper
Hesperia comma Linnaeus

DISTRIBUTION: Europe and temperate Asia to western North America.

FOODPLANTS: Sheep's Fescue (*Festuca ovina*) is the preferred foodplant; captive-bred larvae are reported to take other species of grasses.

GENERAL NOTES

It is reported that this butterfly has declined over recent years in England, completely disappearing from many of its old haunts. Found in chalky areas, it is a localized species which is confined to the chalk hills and downs of southern England. The adult butterflies feed on the nectar of plants, particularly thistles, which are common in its habitat.

The Silver-spotted Skipper is similar to the Large Skipper, but is a duller colour, and the silver spotting on the underside makes recognition relatively simple. The butterflies are on the wing from early August until around the end of the month. The best time to look for them is in the middle two weeks of August.

The females lay their eggs soon after emergence, on the stems and blades of grasses. The yellow eggs, if seen enlarged, are quite different from those of other Skippers, which have the appearance of flat-ended spheres. Eggs of the Silver-spotted Skipper are shaped like upended teacups, with flat tops and rimmed bases which are stuck firmly to the foodplant. As they spend the winter in open ground on blades of grass, the tapered shape could well be an evolutionary adaptation.

The eggs hatch in March, and the dull green larvae draw several blades of grass together with silk, hiding by day and feeding mostly at night. They pupate in late June or early July, constructing cocoons close to the ground, which are made up of fine grasses and silk. Inside, the caterpillar sheds its final skin, and the yellowish chrysalis is loose inside its shelter.

Grizzled Skipper
Pyrgus malvae Linnaeus

DISTRIBUTION: Europe, Asia to Soviet–Chinese border.

FOODPLANTS: Wild Strawberry (*Fragaria vesca*) and Bramble (*Rubus fruticosus*) are the principal foodplants; Raspberry (*Rubus idaeus*) is also taken.

GENERAL NOTES
The Grizzled Skipper is a common species in Britain, being well distributed in England and Wales. Scrubland, sheltered grassy banks and marginal woodlands are favourite haunts of this species, where it visits various flowers in search of nectar, or settles with wings flat to bask in the sunshine. The butterflies will also spend long periods settled on dead flower heads, often roosting in this way at night. They rest with their wings folded back, an attitude which is more characteristic of moths than butterflies, and in this position they are very difficult to spot. Like many other butterflies, they are territorial, and tend to be somewhat aggressive towards other butterflies which venture near.

The females lay their eggs singly on the upperside of leaves. The caterpillars spin a silken cover under which they feed; when large enough, the whole leaf is drawn together for extra protection. They are basically green in colour, with a purplish tinge on the back, and also a faint broad pale striping.

The larva spins a flimsy cocoon at the base of the foodplant, amongst the grasses, and fine bristles on the pupa hold it firmly inside. The pupal wing cases and face are pale grey, with the brown eyes easily visible; the rest of the chrysalis is also brown.

Unlike most of the Skippers, this species progresses through its larval growth to pupate in July, and some individuals will emerge in August to produce a second brood. Second brood larvae pupate in October, so that both broods spend the winter in the pupal stage. Because of this, the adults are ready to emerge earlier than other Skippers. This early emergence, combined with a fast larval growth, allows the production of the second brood.

Dingy Skipper
Erynnis tages Linnaeus

DISTRIBUTION: Europe across Russia to China.

FOODPLANT: The only foodplant is Birdsfoot Trefoil (*Lotus corniculatus*).

GENERAL NOTES

The Dingy Skipper is a common species in the British Isles, well distributed in England and Wales; localized colonies can also be found in Scotland and western Ireland. This butterfly has a similar lifestyle to that of the Grizzled Skipper, and frequents many different kinds of terrain. It has been observed in sheltered quarries and sloping scrublands, and also on raised, exposed sections of disused railway track. When disturbed, it has a habit of flying up at speed, often against the wind, and settling only a short distance away; this manoeuvre can be repeated several times.

The females lay eggs on the terminal growth of the foodplant. On hatching, the larva draws several leaves together with silk, under which it feeds. When the shelter is partly eaten, it moves on to a fresh patch and constructs another one.

The caterpillar is short and dumpy, with narrow green segments and a black head. It feeds in the same manner until the final instar, then, towards the end of August, it constructs a stronger shelter in which it overwinters. In the following spring it quickly attains full growth, finally pupating towards the end of March.

Some larvae pupate in July, and give rise to a partial second brood. These larvae are less mature, taking a little longer to attain full growth. Consequently, the generations probably alternate in producing the partial second brood.

PIERIDAE:
Whites and Sulphurs

This is a large family with a worldwide distribution and has almost 2,000 species, of which six are indigenous to the British Isles; if extinct and migrant species are counted, the number increases to 11.

Many species of this family have migratory tendencies, and on occasion their numbers can reach pest proportions, as with the Large White. The majority of Pierids are white or yellow, and many have black markings. The members of the most colourful genus, *Delias*, have an almost painted appearance, and are often referred to as Jezebels. The front, or prothoracic legs are fully developed and adapted for walking, and the larvae are usually smooth and without spines. The method of pupation is succincti: the cremaster is fixed to a pad of silk, and a silken girdle around the middle provides extra support. The British species belong to three subfamilies: Dismorphiinae, Coliadinae, and Pierinae.

In the tropics and sub-tropics members of this family breed in great abundance, with adults congregating on damp patches of earth in large flocks taking in moisture. When disturbed the flocks take to the air in clouds, but quickly resettle when the disturbance has gone.

Large White
Pieris brassicae Linnaeus

DISTRIBUTION: Europe, Asia, Himalayas, north Africa.

FOODPLANTS: The cabbage family (*Brassica*) and Nasturtium (*Tropaeolum majus*) are the most popular foodplants; others include Garlic Mustard (*Alliaria petiolata*) and Horse-radish (*Armoracia rusticana*).

GENERAL NOTES

The Large White breeds in large numbers throughout the British Isles, and can reach pest proportions when reinforced by migrants. In late April and May, Large Whites emerge from overwintered pupae. The male is pure white on the topside, with black wingtips and a small black blotch on the leading edge of the hindwing. The undersides of the forewings have yellowish wingtips, slightly suffused with black and with two black spots in a lateral line. The undersides of the hindwings are heavily suffused with yellow.

The female is slightly larger, with the same markings, but she has the two lateral black spots on the upperside as well as the underside of the forewings.

Bright yellow eggs are laid in clusters on the underside of leaves, and these soon hatch into batches of larvae. They are gregarious feeders, and can often be seen as a row of heads protruding from the edge of a partly eaten leaf, all moving simultaneously as they feed.

The familiar larvae are yellowish green, peppered with blotches and spots which form thick bands down the body. If disturbed, they wave their heads vigorously from side to side, and vomit pungent green liquid in quite large quantities.

The caterpillars are very prone to attack from the parasitic wasp *Apanteles glomeratus*, and whole broods can be affected. The wasp larvae feed within the body of the host and pupate as a batch of tiny yellow cocoons beside the withering and dying caterpillar.

When mature, the caterpillars move away from the foodplants for pupation. A favourite site is under a window-ledge or the top of a doorway. When negotiating vertical surfaces, the larvae spin a criss-cross trail of silk to obtain an easy footing. They pupate, fixed to the substrate by the cremaster, and girdled. The pupae are yellowish green, and peppered with dark spots. A summer brood soon emerges, much brighter in colour than the spring brood; these butterflies occasionally produce a third brood in exceptional summers.

Small White

Pieris rapae Linnaeus

DISTRIBUTION: Europe, throughout North America, Australia, New Zealand, Asia to Japan.

FOODPLANTS: All the cabbage family (*Brassica*), and as listed for *Pieris brassicae*.

GENERAL NOTES

The Small White is a very successful species, and when introduced by accident into New Zealand in 1930 it soon became a pest over much of the country. The same happened in Australia, nine years later. In the British Isles it is widespread, even occurring in the north of Scotland.

This butterfly can be seen on the wing as early as March, searching for spring flowers in the countryside. The female is double-spotted on the forewings, even in the paler spring brood, but the male's spotting and black wingtips are diminished.

Females lay singly on the foodplants over a wide area, selecting many plants on which they place just a few eggs. This method is highly successful, resulting in a wide distribution of the species. The caterpillars progress through five instars to attain full growth. They usually move away from the foodplant to pupate, often favouring the same situations as *P. brassicae*, but they will occasionally pupate on the foodplant. At this stage, the caterpillar is a dull green, lightly covered with very short pale hairs. On each side of the spiracles there are small yellow blotches, and each spiracle is ringed with a fine black circle. This creates a yellow and black pattern that runs lengthways down each side of the body. Because the head is also green, the larva is camouflaged more effectively than its larger cousin, *P. brassicae*.

The chrysalis is pale greenish brown, fixed to the substrate by the cremaster, and girdled, usually upside down. The butterflies emerge towards the end of August, and these summer brood adults are very much brighter than their predecessors. The male now has a bold spot, and often two

29

on the top and underside of the forewings, and all the markings on the female are more clearly defined. In long, warm seasons a third brood is produced in September, but finally hibernation is in the pupal form.

Green-veined White
Pieris napi Linnaeus

DISTRIBUTION: Europe across Asia to Japan, north Africa, North America (Alaska to Labrador, south from Montana to Arizona, the Lake States, New York).

FOODPLANTS: This butterfly feeds on Cruciferae species, Garlic Mustard (*Alliaria petiolata*), Lady's Smock (*Cardamine pratensis*), Horse-radish (*Armoracia rusticana*), and others.

GENERAL NOTES
The Green-veined White is a very common species, well distributed throughout the British Isles.

This butterfly overwinters in the pupal form, and the adults emerge in March and April. It has the characteristic jaunty flight of the Pierids, and will feed from many of the spring and summer flowers. Buddleia and lavender (particularly the latter) will often tempt this butterfly to linger in a garden, and it will bask in the sunshine with wings half-open when not feeding.

In May, the females seek out their foodplants, and lay their pale yellow eggs singly on the underside of the leaves. The larvae are solitary, and grow rapidly to full maturity in June. They are two-tone green in colour, pale and yellowish on the underside but darker on the topside. Running lengthwise down each side of the body is a row of small yellow spots, one to each segment. The coloration gives good camouflage.

When ready, the caterpillars move away from the foodplant to pupate amongst the undergrowth. The pupa is usually found on a stem, in an upright position, fixed by the tail and girdled. They are very well camouflaged by the pale green colouring, and their broken outline is lost in the surrounding foliage.

Some of these pupae will remain dormant for 10 months; others emerge in July to form a summer brood. These butterflies are much brighter than the spring brood, and their markings are sharper. Eggs laid by these butterflies form pupae by the end of August. The adults live for about six weeks, and many of the spring brood are still flying when the later brood begins to emerge. These, combined with a few migrants which also appear, give the species a flying period lasting from April until the end of August.

Wood White

Leptidea sinapis Linnaeus

DISTRIBUTION: Central and southern Europe through Russia to Caucasus Mountains.

FOODPLANTS: Tuberous Pea (*Lathyrus tuberosus*) is the usual foodplant. They will take other vetches and peas, and also Birdsfoot Trefoil (*Lotus corniculatus*).

GENERAL NOTES
In Britain the Wood White is distributed from central Wales to the Cotswolds, down through Hampshire to the coast. A few colonies can be found in the eastern counties, and they are most abundant in Cornwall. Wherever they appear, the colonies are very localized; there is also an Irish race.

The adults are out in May, when they can be seen feeding from woodland flowers. They have a weak, delicate flight, staying hidden when winds rise above a gentle breeze, and rarely venture away from the protection of woodlands. They are often found with wings folded, or basking in broken sunlight in woodland rides and glades.

The Wood White is not a very inspiring butterfly: its colour is a rather insipid greyish white, and the markings are pale and variable. The narrow wings have a delicate fragility, even for a butterfly, and the body is black and slender.

The females lay eggs singly on the underside of leaves, and the eggs hatch after about a week. The first brood larvae feed through four instars, pupating in July. They are light green in colour with a pale yellow stripe down each side of the body; a narrow band of skin above the stripe has a faint tinge of blue, and the caterpillar is generally bright in appearance.

The caterpillar selects an upright stem for pupation amongst the undergrowth, and the chrysalis is fixed by the tail and girdled. It has a slender, well-shaped appearance, with yellowish green coloration, and the wing cases are picked out in pale green.

Adults will occasionally emerge in August, producing a partial second brood, and these caterpillars have an extra instar before pupating in September to hibernate.

Orange Tip

Anthocharis cardamines Linnaeus

DISTRIBUTION: Europe through temperate Asia to China.

FOODPLANTS: Lady's Smock (*Cardamine pratensis*) is the principal foodplant; also Garlic Mustard (*Alliaria petiolata*). Other species of Cruciferae are used, but the former are most favoured. In captivity, Sweet Rocket (*Hesperis matronalis*) is an excellent alternative foodplant.

GENERAL NOTES

The Orange Tip is a very common species in Britain, widespread in England and Wales. It also occurs in the north of Scotland as far as Inverness and in Ireland. This butterfly is associated with the best weather of the year, being single-brooded and on the wing from May to July. Only the male has the brilliant orange tips to the wings, and the upper and undersides are equally attractive. The orange is brighter on the top, but the beautiful mossy green coloration is only found on the underside.

The eggs are laid singly towards the top of the foodplant, on leaf tips and terminal growth; at first they are white, but they soon turn bright orange. This is the best time to collect them for captive rearing, because their colour makes them easy to spot.

The caterpillar is pale green, and each side is suffused with a broad white band. Almost invariably, they will be on *C. pratensis*, and the larvae rest along the length of seed pods. It takes a well-trained eye to pick them out. Several eggs may be laid on a single plant, but the cannibalistic tendencies of the larvae mean that usually only one will survive; it is therefore wise to remember to separate captive stock.

Brimstone

Gonepteryx rhamni Linnaeus

DISTRIBUTION: Canary Isles through Europe and Asia to Japan.

FOODPLANTS: Buckthorn (*Rhamnus cathartica*) and Alder Buckthorn (*Frangula alnus*) are the only foodplants.

GENERAL NOTES

The Brimstone can be seen in practically any type of habitat, from gardens to woodlands. They fly long distances, often seen miles from an area which contains their foodplant. In Britain they are abundant in England, common in Wales, but scarce north of Shropshire. They are also fairly common in Ireland.

The Brimstone will venture out of hibernation as soon as the weather permits, which can be as early as February, but cold weather will usually force them back into hibernation.

The males seem always to be on the wing at the onset of the season, and will fly through one's field of vision quite quickly, soaring over hedges and across gardens. Later in the season they are less energetic, feeding lazily for long periods and settling out of the direct sun with wings folded. In fact, they dislike very hot days, often spending long periods under a leaf in the shade.

The male is a very bright yellow, whereas the female is paler with a greenish tinge. Both sexes have darker undersides, and the females are often mistaken for the Large White by vegetable gardeners (but not by butterfly enthusiasts!).

The females lay their eggs on buckthorn, even before the buds have opened, and continue to lay until it is in leaf. On hatching, the larvae keep to the rib of the leaf, pressed flat and excellently camouflaged. They are very similar to the Small White larvae.

The caterpillars have five instars, taking about four to five weeks to reach full growth. At this stage they move away from the foodplant to pupate in the undergrowth.

The chrysalis is girdled, very leaf-like and difficult to spot. The fresh adults emerge in July and August, and could well be flying with their parents.

They move away from the foodplant to pupate amongst the undergrowth, and the chrysalis is fixed by the tail and girdled. The pupae are quite unusual, being tapered at the head and tail to fine points of about equal proportions, and, like, the larvae, they are very slender.

LYCAENIDAE:
Blues, Coppers and Hairstreaks

This family comprises about 3,000 species, widely distributed throughout the world, and it contains some of the smallest butterflies with the most dazzling colours.

Species found in the British Isles belong to two subfamilies: the Theclinae, or Hairstreaks, and the Lycaeninae, the Blues and Coppers. Even with their brilliant coloration, these butterflies are not easily spotted and non-enthusiasts may rarely, if ever, see them in the wild, even if they live in country areas where the butterflies are abundant.

The larvae of most British Blues feed on Leguminosae and other low-growing vegetation such as dock and sorrel (*Rumex*), and they have a characteristic woodlouse shape with tapered tail and small head. The segmental divisions are usually well-defined, and their coloration gives excellent camouflage.

The topside coloration of males is usually various shades of bright blue, but the females are much less conspicuous in sombre shades of brown. The undersides of both sexes are very similar, being spotted and patterned with orange crescents and broken lines on a background of silvery white, tinged with brown or blue.

Very little is known about the Hairstreaks, but most of these are localized and difficult to find. The larvae are woodlouse-shaped, mostly feeding from trees, and always concealing themselves by boring into leaf buds and flower heads. They are nearly all single-brooded, probably owing to the recently discovered fact that trees produce poisons in their leaves when attacked by insects; caterpillars eating older growth would be unable to grow properly, and could even die. Therefore, although the larvae would have ample good weather and abundant foodplants, the eggs lie dormant throughout the summer for eight or nine months. They hatch the following season, even before the spring buds are open, and feed from their contents; as these buds open, the larvae mature fully and pupate before the trees have a chance to retaliate.

Both male and female Coppers are beautifully coloured, the males brighter but the females superbly marked, and the brilliance of the male Large Copper is truly magnificent. The original Large Copper, *Lycaena dispar dispar*, has been extinct in Britain since the 1850s, but the introduced species, *L. dispar botavus*, is virtually identical, although it would probably not survive without the help of the wardens on the nature reserve where it breeds.

Black Hairstreak

Strymonidia pruni Linnaeus

DISTRIBUTION: Central and eastern Europe to Asia.

FOODPLANTS: Blackthorn or Sloe (*Prunus spinosa*) is the only wild foodplant. Captive larvae will take various plum leaves.

GENERAL NOTES

This little butterfly is a rare and endangered species in England, confined to a few localized colonies stretching from Oxfordshire, north-east towards the Wash for about 60 miles. The Black Hairstreak frequents mature oak woodlands, containing old blackthorn thickets where they breed.

It is often mistaken for the White Letter Hairstreak (*S. w-album*) (see below), but the distinguishing features become apparent if the two are seen side by side. The Black Hairstreak is slightly larger than the White Letter Hairstreak, and has marginal orange spots on the upperside of the hindwing; the female also has these orange spots to a lesser and more variable degree on the topside of the forewing. This orange spotting is absent on *S. w-album*. On the underside, the marginal orange spotting on the hindwing is much broader in *S. pruni* and this gradually fades into the forewings in both male and female; there is no orange spotting beneath the forewings of *S. w-album*.

Most of the Hairstreaks, especially *S. pruni* and *S. w-album*, are particularly fond of wild privet flowers. When not feeding, however, the butterflies tend to settle well out of sight and reach. They will alight on top of tall bracken with their wings closed, rubbing them together in a slow, backward and forward motion characteristic of Hairstreaks.

The butterflies are on the wing towards the end of July, and lay their eggs on the thin twigs of last year's growth. Seen highly magnified, the eggs are flat and spiny with an indentation in the top. They are quite inconspicuous on the twigs, and remain dormant throughout the winter, hatching in the following April.

The caterpillars are curious, woodlouse-shaped creatures with a double lateral row of tiny humps, two to each segment, which diminish in size towards the head and tail. They are pale green in colour, with a red tinge to each of the humps along the back. On both sides of each segment are two pale, diagonal stripes. It is therefore an interesting little caterpillar, both in colour and shape.

The larvae pupate in early June, securely girdled and fixed by the cremaster on to the side of a twig, looking more like blemishes on the tree than pupae. The adults emerge after about two weeks, and they fly until early July.

White-letter Hairstreak
Strymonidia w-album Knoch

DISTRIBUTION: North Europe and Japan.

FOODPLANTS: Wych Elm (*Ulmus glabra*) and the Common Elm (*Ulmus procera*).

GENERAL NOTES
This species is not common in Britain, but occurs in many localized colonies throughout England and Wales. Some

confusion arises between this species and *S. pruni* (see above), but the distinguishing features are discussed under *S. pruni*.

The White-letter Hairstreak has a wider range of habitat than its rarer relation and, although woodlands are a favoured haunt, it will breed in more open situations if the foodplant is present. Country lanes, even lone trees on scrubland could attract this butterfly. It can even be tempted into a garden bordering on a breeding site by buddleia, and will feed from sticky secretions that often form on leaves.

This is a single-brooded species, and the adults are first seen on the wing in July and August.

The females lay their eggs on twigs of elm trees. The eggs are quite different from those of *S. pruni*, being flat and black, and very well camouflaged. They remain dormant throughout the winter, and hatch in March, when the tiny larvae bore into the unopened buds. As the tree bursts into leaf, the larvae continue to feed on tender young growth and also the flowers.

The caterpillar is very much like *S. pruni*, but is a more yellowish green, and it has just one diagonal dark stripe on both sides of each segment. Four instars are required to attain full growth, and the caterpillar finally pupates under a leaf or on a twig, succincti, held by the tail and girdled.

It is not yet clear how seriously this species has been affected by the spread of Dutch Elm Disease, but it will almost certainly have suffered. Wych elm, however, has not been destroyed to the same extent as the common elm, and this will hopefully aid its survival.

Brown Hairstreak
Thecla betulae Linnaeus

DISTRIBUTION: Central and north Europe, northern Asia to the Pacific.

FOODPLANTS: Blackthorn or Sloe (*Prunus spinosa*) is the only wild foodplant, but captive larvae will take plum.

GENERAL NOTES

The Brown Hairstreak is a localized species in the British Isles, found in the Midland and southern counties of England, with some colonies in Wales and Ireland.

Their frequent habitat which is similar to that of *Strymonidia w-album* (see above) is large woodland clearings and open hedgerow situations, provided blackthorn is available.

The butterflies are secretive, hiding in trees and in the canopy of hedges, making sighting difficult. They remain settled with wings folded, and will only fly in bright, warm sunshine.

The female has more colour than the male, with a large orange patch on the forewings and a little more on the short tails and trailing margins. The male is almost devoid of orange, with just a faint patch beside the discoidal spots, and beside the tails. The underside of both male and female is a vivid russet brown, with black and white streaks running together across both wings.

The butterflies fly from August until early October, producing eggs soon after emergence. The ova is the best form in which to obtain this species for captive breeding. Females lay their eggs mostly on or near terminal growth. The eggs are greyish white in colour, and quite conspicuous to the trained eye. They remain affixed and dormant from August to late April or early May, at which time the tiny larvae hatch and eat their eggshells. The caterpillars are typical of the Hairstreaks, being green in colour, and take about seven weeks to attain full growth.

Pupation is slightly unusual: the larva spins a cremastal pad of silk, and firmly grips the pad between the claspers. The caterpillar sheds the final skin down to the lower abdomen, where it stops. The tail end and cremaster stay in the remains of the last skin like a light socket, and without girdle support.

Only one brood is produced each season, and the adults emerge after about four weeks.

Green Hairstreak

Callophrys rubi Linnaeus

DISTRIBUTION: Europe and Asia.

FOODPLANTS: This species will feed on a host of foodplants, the principal one being Gorse (*Ulex europaeus*). Among other foodplants are Birdsfoot Trefoil (*Lotus corniculatus*), Dogwood (*Swida sanguinea*), Buckthorn (*Rhamnus cathartica*), and Rock Rose (*Helianthemum nummularium*).

GENERAL NOTES

The Green Hairstreak is evenly distributed throughout England and Wales, and is fairly common in some of the Hebrides and in Ireland. Open situations adjacent to woodland are ideal habitat, especially if the terrain is rough, scrubby and dotted with gorse bushes.

This butterfly is a single-brooded species, emerging in May, and flies until the end of June. It is therefore on the wing when the bluebells are in bloom, and a Green Hairstreak can often be seen on a flower head, flopped over to one side as though blown over by the wind.

This is the only green butterfly native to Britain, and, unlike other Hairstreaks, it will spend long periods close to the ground, either feeding from flowers or settled with wings folded.

The only marking in the green on this species is a white hair-streak across the hind wing. It can be sharp and clear, or thin and broken, diminished to a few spots or completely absent.

Females lay their eggs on terminal growth, and also on the flower heads of the foodplant, and the larvae progress through four instars to maturity. Captive larvae have to be separated because of cannibalism.

The caterpillars are typical of their race, being green, but they do not pupate on the foodplant; instead, they move down to the ground and pupate loose amongst the grasses. The chrysalis will lie dormant for 10 months, finally emerging in May.

This species is the only Hairstreak to overwinter as pupae; all the other species overwinter as eggs.

Purple Hairstreak

Quercusia quercus Linnaeus

DISTRIBUTION: Europe to Asia Minor.

FOODPLANT: Common Oak (*Quercus robur*) is the only foodplant.

GENERAL NOTES

The Purple Hairstreak is one of the more common species in the British Isles, well distributed in England and Wales south of the Midlands, but more localized further north as far as Ross. It is also found in pockets in Ireland.

This species emerges in July, flying throughout August and into September. It is most frequently found in old oak woodlands, but can occasionally be seen in clearings and woodland rides, feeding from sticky leaf secretions. Most of this butterfly's adult life is spent high on the wing, quite often in small flocks.

The male's wings are mostly purple, with black margins, but the female is much darker, with purple patches only on the base of the forewings.

One brood is produced each season, and the eggs are laid soon after the adults appear. The females usually lay at the base of leaf buds, and when the larva hatches it bores straight into the bud. The green contents are eaten, and the larva then moves on to another bud. As the leaves begin to appear, the larva continues to feed from the tender young shoots, finally pupating towards the end of May.

Pupation is involuti (loose); larvae will pupate in cracks and crevices of the bark, or on the ground amongst decaying leaves and bracken. The chrysalis is very dark green in colour, and the adult emerges after about five weeks.

Small Copper
Lycaena phlaeas Linnaeus

DISTRIBUTION: Europe, north Africa, temperate Asia to Japan, eastern North America.

FOODPLANTS: Dock and Sorrel (*Rumex*) are the two foodplants.

GENERAL NOTES

The Small Copper is very common in Britain throughout England and Wales, occurring to a lesser degree in Scotland, as far north as Orkney. It is also quite common in Ireland.

These butterflies prefer exposed areas, but also have a particular liking for small, sheltered spots, such as the corner of a field which may trap the sun. Sunlit quarries and open waste ground, even in towns, will attract this beautiful butterfly.

Flowers of the daisy family are most favoured by the adults, especially those which flower in late spring or summer.

The Small Copper is extremely territorial, chasing off intruding butterflies and other insects; the same individuals may be seen for several days within a small area.

The female is a little larger than the male, and her wings are more rounded; she also has rudimentary tails, which are absent in the male. They fly in rapid bursts from flower to flower, and turn like ballet dancers whilst feeding. They will also bask for a short while in the sunshine, on flowers and grasses or on the ground.

Three broods are produced in a normal season, and the first butterflies are out towards the end of April or early May. Greyish white eggs are laid on any part of the foodplant, and the female will often lay two eggs before moving off.

The caterpillars are green, the same shade as the foodplants. Segment divisions are well defined, and they have a brown dorsal line. Their legs are tinted with pink, as is the lower part of the body, just above the prolegs.

The larvae will feed from the edge of leaves, or perforate

them, progressing through five instars before pupation. The chrysalis is brown and quite pale, the wing cases streaked with black. The pupa is girdled and fixed by the cremaster, usually under a leaf or on a stem in the undergrowth.

Eggs laid in July will normally produce larvae which hibernate when partly grown; however, in good seasons a partial fourth brood may occur, giving rise to more larvae in October. These join the earlier brood in hibernation, and produce the next spring adults.

Large Copper
Lycaena dispar Haworth

DISTRIBUTION: West and central Europe to Soviet–Chinese border.

FOODPLANT: Great Water Dock (*Rumex hydrolapathum*)

GENERAL NOTES

Sadly, this beautiful butterfly remains in Britain only in the form of set specimens; it has been extinct in Britain since about 1850. The Dutch subspecies (*L. dispar batavus*) was introduced to Woodwalton Fen, England in 1915, and they still survive today, but without the care of the fen wardens it is thought they would probably die out.

The male is a brilliant copper colour, with jet black wing borders. The discoidal spots on upper and hindwings show as a black spot in the copper. The female is better marked, and larger; the copper colour is reduced to a bar towards the outer margin of the hindwings, and the forewing is heavily bordered with black spots across the wings, and more towards the wing bases.

The larvae feed on Great Water Dock (*Rumex hydrolapathum*), and are bright green. They hibernate as partly grown larvae, amongst the old foodplant, and feed up in the spring, pupating in June. The nut-brown pupa is girdled and fixed by the tail to a stem away from the foodplant.

Common Blue

Polyommatus icarus Rottemburg

DISTRIBUTION: Canary Isles, north Africa, Europe to temperate Asia.

FOODPLANTS: Birdsfoot Trefoil (*Lotus corniculatus*) is the principal foodplant, but they will also take clover, medick and other Leguminosae.

GENERAL NOTES

As its name suggests, this species is the commonest of the Blues in the British Isles; it is abundant throughout Britain, and common in Ireland wherever its foodplant occurs. Rough, open grasslands and scrublands, especially on sloping hillsides, are suitable habitat for the Common Blue, but it prefers chalk or limestone. Disused railway tracks and old quarries are often frequented.

The male is bright blue with a hint of violet, edged with a black border of hair's breadth around the outer margin. With the exception of the leading edge, a line of pure white hair protrudes from this black border, forming an unbroken fringe. The female is brown with a sprinkling of blue scales; however, this can vary, and on some females the blue is extensive. On the outer margin of the hindwings, the female has a row of black spots, half surrounded on the inside by orange crescents. These extend in a diminished form into the forewings. The markings on this species are very variable.

This is a double-brooded species, but the second brood is only partial. The female lays eggs on the upperside of leaves towards the end of May, and the larvae hatch in June.

The green caterpillars have a darker, ridged back, and they are covered with short, brownish hair. Full growth is attained in five instars, and they pupate towards the end of July. The chrysalis is green and formed loose inside a flimsy cocoon at the base of the foodplant. The head and pupal wing cases are tinged with buff.

Only a percentage of this brood pupate; the remainder are slower to grow, and overwinter at the third instar. Those which do pupate emerge towards the end of August, and soon produce larvae. These in turn join those of the first brood in hibernation.

Small Blue
Cupido minimus Fuessly

DISTRIBUTION: Europe through Asia to Soviet–Chinese border.

FOODPLANT: Kidney Vetch (*Anthyllis vulneraria*) is the only foodplant of this species.

GENERAL NOTES

This, the smallest butterfly occurring in Britain, is quite common in the southern counties of England, and also in the Cotswolds. A few colonies can be found in central Scotland, although very localized, and also in Ireland.

It occurs in small, isolated colonies on rough ground, often in sheltered hollows. Favourite haunts can be sunlit railway embankments, where miniature landslides have produced sheltered shallow crevasses which have re-vegetated. These tiny colonies can easily be passed-by unnoticed.

The male is slightly smaller than the female, very dark in colour, with a flush of blue in the wings. The female has a fatter body, and little or no blue colouring at all. The underside of both sexes is, in complete contrast, pale greyish white or silver, with a blue tinge towards the wing bases. There is also a variable number of spots across fore- and hindwings, and these are black, encircled with white.

The Small Blue is a double-brooded species, but, again, the second brood is only partial. Females lay single eggs on the flowers of kidney vetch, and the caterpillars promptly bore into the flower heads. These larvae are yellowish brown in colour, with a darker lateral band along the back, and are covered with fine brownish bristles. The caterpillars grow quite fast, and attain full growth by August. Some will now go into hibernation, drawing several dead flower heads together with silk to form a shelter. Others pupate, girdled to the foodplant, and emerge as adults within about 12 days. The larvae of this partial second brood hibernate with those remaining of the first brood, and together form the next season's early adults.

The chrysalis is whitish grey, with dark lateral spots on the dorsal area, and dark streaking in the pupal wing cases.

Large Blue
Maculinea arion Linnaeus

DISTRIBUTION: Europe across Russia and Siberia to China.

FOODPLANTS: Wild Thyme (*Thymus praecox*), is the foodplant until the third instar; thereafter the food comprises the larvae of *Myrmica* ants.

GENERAL NOTES

No book on butterflies would be complete without some mention of the Large Blue and its strange life cycle. The species is now reported to be extinct in England, and one can only hope that a colony may still exist in some unknown location.

The Large Blue was once widely distributed in England in the Cotswolds, Devon and Cornwall. Its bizarre, although not unique, association with ants was discovered in 1915 by Capt. E. B. Purefoy, whilst assisting F. W. Frowhawk.

It is a single-brooded species, and emerges in July, depending on the location. The females lay their bluish white eggs singly on the flower buds of wild thyme. On hatching, the larvae move into the flower heads, where they feed from the flowers rather than the leaves.

The larva is a pale brownish pink, with four lateral rows of long curved hairs. The body is peppered with tiny, dark brown spots, and the head is also brown.

The caterpillar begins to grow and shed its skin as normal until the fourth instar, when it becomes restless, finally falling or wandering off the foodplant. At this stage, even if carefully retrieved and placed on the tenderest flower, it would refuse to feed. The wandering caterpillar is eventually discovered by an ant of the genus *Myrmica*, of which there are about 10 different species. The ant begins to investigate its find, the caterpillar remaining motionless to avoid attack. The caterpillar then gradually contracts its ʾody, and in so doing compresses a gland on the tenth segment. This secretes honeydew, a sweet liquid, and the ant immediately consumes this, often returning to its nest and later reappearing to collect more. An hour or more can elapse, and often more than one ant will return from the nest to milk the caterpillar of its honeydew; finally the caterpillar arches its back, which allows the ant to seize it and carry it off, unharmed.

The caterpillar is placed in the brood chamber of the ants' nest, where it begins the second stage of its larval life, feeding on ant larvae.

Within six weeks, the caterpillar trebles in size, altering considerably as a result of its new diet, and, as winter approaches, it hibernates in the ants' nest.

The following spring it continues to feed on the ant brood until ready to pupate, which it does, loose, in the brood chamber. Three weeks later, the butterfly emerges and, while its wings are still soft and damp, it crawls up through the nest and out into the undergrowth, where it hangs upside down to expand its wings.

Chalkhill Blue

Lysandra coridon Poda

DISTRIBUTION: Europe.

FOODPLANTS: Horseshoe Vetch (*Hippocrepis comosa*) is the principal foodplant. Captive larvae will also accept Birdsfoot Trefoil (*Lotus corniculatus*), Kidney Vetch (*Anthyllis vulneraria*) and other Leguminosae.

GENERAL NOTES
In Britain the Chalkhill Blue is confined to the Cotswolds, and counties of central and south-eastern England. It frequents chalky or limestone areas and, where colonies occur, their numbers can run into hundreds.

The silvery blue colour in the male of this species distinguishes it from the other Blues, as it is pale by comparison. It has a black spot between each vein on the outer margins, which are suffused with broad black borders. On the hindwings, this border is narrower, and the spots are separate from it. The female is very dark, with the spotting just visible on the forewings, but on the hindwings the spots are encircled with pale brown, making them clearer. The underside of both sexes is silvery grey with a brownish tint, the female being slightly darker, but the spotting is extremely variable. It should be noted that this is an extremely variable butterfly, and large collections exist which consist purely of Chalkhill Blue aberrations.

The middle of July is the time when the adults appear, and they fly for about seven to eight weeks. It is a single-brooded species. The eggs are laid on and near the larval foodplant, amongst the grasses. The larva forms inside the eggshell, and then lies dormant for about seven months, finally hatching in early April.

The caterpillars are green with a ridge running down each side and joining at the tail. There is also a double lateral ridge of tiny humps running almost the whole length of the body. The ridge and humps are tinged with yellow, which increases in intensity as the flowers of the foodplant develop; this gives the larvae superb camouflage.

The caterpillars finally pupate on the ground, loose, in the middle of June.

Adonis Blue

Lysandra bellargus Rottemburg

DISTRIBUTION: Europe to Iraq and Iran.

FOODPLANT: Horseshoe Vetch (*Hippocrepis comosa*) is the only known foodplant.

GENERAL NOTES

The Adonis Blue has declined in Britain over the past decade, disappearing from many of its old haunts. It is now a very localized species, only in southern counties of England.

This is a double-brooded species, which is found on chalk and limestone. It often shares its habitat with the Chalkhill Blue, but is not as common.

The Adonis Blue may be confused with the Common Blue (*Polyommatus icarus*); however, the blue coloration of the male is much brighter, and the wing veining cuts through the white marginal fringe, making the veins appear extended; on *P. icarus* the white fringe is unbroken. The underside of the female *L. bellargus* has a browner tinge than *P. icarus*, but it could be confused with the Chalkhill Blue, *L. coridon*. However, the suffused blue scaling on the topside of the female *L. coridon* is of the paler, powder blue, characteristic of that species, while on *L. bellargus* it is a bright iridescent blue.

The butterflies are out in May, and the females lay their eggs on the leaves of the foodplant. On hatching, the larvae keep to the underside of the leaf, perforating it and taking the edges. The mature caterpillar is bright green, and the segmental divisions are clearly defined. They have yellow lateral stripes on the back and sides, and the body is lightly coated with pale brown hairs.

When ready, the caterpillar makes its way to the base of the foodplant, and pupates loose on the ground in a very flimsy covering of silken strands. The fresh chrysalis is greenish brown with green wing cases, but after a short time the whole shell turns light brown.

Butterflies of the spring brood have been gone for about six weeks when the second brood appears in late August, and these adults only last for approximately three weeks. Larvae produced by the second brood hibernate in their second or third instar, depending on temperature, and lie affixed to a pad of silk under a leaf of the foodplant.

Brown Argus

Aricia agestis Denis and Schiffermüller

DISTRIBUTION: Europe to Iran, Siberia and Soviet–Chinese border.

FOODPLANTS: Rock Rose (*Helianthemum nummularium*) and Storksbill (*Erodium cicutarium*).

GENERAL NOTES

In Britain the Brown Argus is well distributed in the Cotswolds, East Anglia and the central and southern counties of England, with a few localized colonies in north and south Wales.

These butterflies are out in May and June, frequenting grassy banks, old quarries and scrublands, and they are often seen in the company of other species which enjoy the same habitat.

There can be some confusion in trying to distinguish the Brown Argus from the female Common Blue (*Polyommatus icarus*) (see page 44), especially as they are found in similar types of terrain. However, *P. icarus* is slightly larger and, of course, the male of *P. icarus* is blue, which causes no problems. There are no blue scales at all on *A. agestis,* whereas most female *P. icarus* have some blue, albeit the slighest sprinkling of scales. The underside of *A. agestis* is duller, with a brownish tint, and the reddish orange spots in the outer margins on both upper and underside of male and female are larger and more clearly defined, especially on the forewing. The upperside of the forewing has a black discal spot and on the underside of the wings there are black spots encircled with white.

The Brown Argus is a double-brooded species. Females lay on the underside of the leaves, and the caterpillars hatch within about seven days. The larvae feed up to full growth through five instars and, when ready, draw several leaves together with a few strands of silk and pupate loose inside. The second brood begins to emerge by the end of July and produces larvae by the end of August. The caterpillar is green with pinkish lateral lines on the back and each side. It has a shiny black head, and a smattering of short spines.

At the third instar, these second-brood larvae affix themselves along the rib of a leaf, and hibernate until the following March, finally pupating in April. The chrysalis is a yellowish green with pink bands on the back and sides of the body; the wing cases are smooth and glossy.

Aricia artaxerxes Fabricius
Similar in appearance to the Brown Argus is the Northern Brown Argus, which occurs in Scotland and northern England and across northern Europe. For many years this was considered to be a subspecies of *A. agestis*, but it is now known to be a distinct and separate species, *A. artaxerxes*.

The Northern Brown Argus can be distinguished from the Brown Argus by the blind white spots on the underside of the wings, instead of black spots encircled by white. The discal spot on the upperside of the forewing is pure white. This northern species is single-brooded.

Silver-studded Blue

Plebejus argus Linnaeus

DISTRIBUTION: Europe, temperate Asia to Japan.

FOODPLANTS: Gorse (*Ulex europaeus*) and Birdsfoot Vetch (*Ornithopus perpusillus*) are two well-used foodplants; broom and heather are also taken.

GENERAL NOTES
In Britain the Silver-studded Blue is widely distributed in England and Wales, but is most common in the central southern counties of England. It is a butterfly which varies greatly according to its location, and there are four subspecies: ssp. *argus argus* is found on heathlands, whilst ssp. *cretaceus* favours chalky downland and is slightly larger. Ssp. *caernensis* is the smallest and is found in north Wales. The male of the latter subspecies has a very narrow black outer margin, and the female has two bright blue flushes at the base of the forewings, with narrower blue flushes towards the orange spots on the hindwings. A further northern subspecies, *masseyi*, was destroyed by fire in 1941; this was similar to *caernensis*, but a little larger. The marginal black border in the male was not as broad as in *argus argus*,

but broader than in *caernensis*, and the blue coloration in the female was much more extensive.

The violet blue and narrower wing shape of this species as a whole clearly distinguish it from other Blues.

It is a single-brooded species, and is on the wing towards the end of July and into the middle of August. During this time, the females lay their eggs on the leaves of the foodplant, and the eggs lie dormant throughout the winter, hatching around the end of March.

The caterpillars are reddish brown with black lateral stripes, and are finely peppered with tiny white spots. The body is covered in short, fine hairs, and the head is black. The larvae undergo five instars to attain full growth, and pupate low down on the foodplant or a nearby stem, girdled and fixed by the cremaster. The chrysalis is pale yellowish green, with paler wing cases; adults emerge after about two weeks.

Holly Blue

Celastrina argiolus Linnaeus

DISTRIBUTION: Europe, north Africa, India, Asia, Japan, Malaysia.

FOODPLANTS: The Holly Blue is unusual in that it has a different foodplant for its two seasonal broods. The spring adults lay their eggs on Holly (*Ilex*), while the summer adults lay on Ivy (*Hedera*). Other reported foodplants are Alder Buckthorn (*Frangula alnus*) and Dogwood (*Swida sanguinea*).

GENERAL NOTES

In the British Isles this species is very common in England and Wales, although its numbers sometimes fluctuate from year to year. In Scotland and Ireland the Holly Blue is more localized and, in some years, scarce. These butterflies frequent open woodland, parks and even gardens where its foodplants occur. It has a spring and a summer brood which vary in colour to a certain extent, and in exceptional years a third brood is also produced.

The first butterflies appear on the wing very early, often at the end of March, and they are easily distinguished from the other Blues. The male is slightly paler than the Common Blue, being almost powder blue, and has a black band extending from the forewing tip (where it is slightly broader) along the outer margin. The female has a much wider band, again thicker at the tip, but extending over about one-third of the wing. The hindwing is dusky on the forward edge, with a narrow black line and black spots along the rear margin. The underside of both male and female is silvery white, with a few variable black spots, and a slight blue tinge towards the base of the wings. Females of this brood lay on young shoots and flower buds of holly. The larvae remain more or less where the egg was laid, feeding to full growth and pupating, fixed by the tail and girdled, under a holly leaf.

The summer brood emerges in July, and there is a marked difference in the females. The male is a little brighter and clearer, but the female has a much more extensive black border, and the hindwing spots are larger, and suffused with the marginal band.

Females of this brood lay most of their eggs on ivy, and these larvae grow much faster in the higher temperature, attaining full growth by early September. The caterpillars are bright yellowish green, with a dark head and tiny white hairs. They pupate on the foodplant and usually remain there over the winter.

In exceptional seasons, some of these pupae emerge in September and produce a third brood, which pupate in November. Adults of this brood are much smaller and paler than their predecessors.

NEMEOBIIDAE:
Metalmarks

This large family of almost 2,000 species is mostly confined to South America. The Duke of Burgundy Fritillary is the only species to be found in Europe.

They are all small butterflies, but vary enormously in shape and colour. The members of one subfamily, Chorinae, have long narrow tails, and those of the subfamily Ancylurinae have metallic colouring which defies description.

The size and shape of many of the Metalmarks could well be confused with Lycaenidae; however, the front or prothoracic legs of the males are under-developed and useless for walking, which suggests a resemblance to Nymphalidae, of which both males and females have reduced forelegs. Perhaps Nemeobiidae are a link between the two.

Duke of Burgundy Fritillary
Hamearis lucina Linnaeus

DISTRIBUTION: Britain, Europe.

FOODPLANTS: Cowslip (*Primula veris*) is the principal foodplant, but they will accept primrose.

GENERAL NOTES
The Duke of Burgundy Fritillary is a fairly localized species in Britain, never seen in large numbers, and appearing more frequently in the southern counties of England. There are also a few colonies in the Lake District and Yorkshire. It is the only member of its family to be found in Europe, and its name is derived from its resemblance to the true Fritillaries.

This butterfly is primarily a woodland species, frequenting open rides and sunny woodland glades, but it will also favour grassy slopes and scrubland where its foodplant may flourish. It is an active little butterfly, rarely staying in one place for very long, and is equally satisfied drinking from a puddle's edge as it is from flowers. When disturbed, it will depart at speed, and because of its small size and dark colouring against the undergrowth, it may prove very difficult to keep in sight.

The adults appear around the middle of May, and remain on the wing for about four weeks. Females lay eggs on the underside of the leaf in small groups of two or three eggs. On hatching, the larvae remain under the leaves and begin to progress through four instars.

The caterpillar is brown with a diagonal stripe on each segment that forms a lateral pattern down each side. It also has a row of spots down the back, and the body is covered in short hairs of light and dark shades. During late summer, the larvae pupate on the underside of leaves, usually on the foodplant.

The pupa is girdled and fixed to a pad of silk by the cremaster. The chrysalis is pale in colour with rows of spots and blotches across each segment, forming a lateral pattern. It remains in this position through the winter, for almost 10 months, producing only one brood each season.

SATYRIDAE: Browns

This family is very closely related to Nymphalidae, and considered by some authorities to be a subfamily. There are only 11 species in the British Isles, but worldwide the numbers are approaching 3,000.

The butterflies have a slow and characteristically erratic flight, and yet some are capable of travelling long distances; and the British population of several species is increased each year by migrants.

The wing veining towards the thorax is swollen, which is a useful method of identification, and the front pair of legs are reduced in size and held up tight against the thorax, as in Nymphalidae.

A characteristic wing marking is the eye-spots (ocelli); practically all carry some vestige of these, and many are very clearly defined, even forming chains.

Many species find strong sunlight either too bright or too hot, and keep to woodland rides and clearings, preferring sunshine filtered through leaves; others stay hidden during the hottest part of the day, and fly in the early morning or evening. They also survive with great success in colder regions and at quite high altitudes.

The larvae are usually smooth and plump, carrying hair rather than spines, and a large proportion are grass feeders.

Small Mountain Ringlet
Erebia epiphron Knoch

DISTRIBUTION: Europe.

FOODPLANTS: Captive larvae will take various species of grasses. In the wild, they prefer Mat Grass (*Nardus stricta*).

GENERAL NOTES

The young enthusiast attempting to obtain a complete British collection finds this species one of the most elusive. The Small Mountain Ringlet must be classed as rare in Britain and it is the only true alpine species to be found here, not usually found below 450m (1,500ft). The only colonies, which are extremely localized, exist in the Lake District and central Scotland.

The butterflies emerge in May and early June, and live for three to four weeks. They have a very delicate appearance, and a weak flight, yet manage to survive in terrain that can only be described as hostile.

The females are slightly larger than the males, and have fatter bodies, but the orange ocelli on the males' wings are a little brighter. Eggs are laid singly on the blades of mat grass, and the tiny larvae feed until August, when they go into hibernation. The caterpillars are characteristic of the grass feeders, being soft-bodied with tapering tails. They have two narrow pale cream lines down each side of the body, but the basic colour is green, blending in with the foodplant.

After hibernation, the larvae continue to feed, completing four instars before finally pupating in May. The caterpillar moves to ground level, and loosely binds a few pieces of vegetation together with fine silk. Under this flimsy protective cover, the larva pupates, unrestrained, loose on the ground. The chrysalis is green in colour, with a finely pointed tail.

Only one brood is produced each year, and the adults will only fly in sunshine, even if the air is warm.

Scotch Argus
Erebia aethiops Esper

DISTRIBUTION: North and central Europe, Asia Minor, Urals, Caucasus.

FOODPLANTS: Purple Moor Grass (*Molinia caerulea*) is the principal foodplant, but captive-bred larvae accept other grasses.

GENERAL NOTES

In Britain the Scotch Argus is well distributed in Scotland, mostly in central and western regions, including some off-shore islands. A few localized colonies can also be found in the far north of England.

The butterflies are found in open, sunny locations such as sheltered hillsides. During August, they are often seen in large numbers.

This species is on the wing towards the end of July, and throughout August. There is little difference in the size of male and female, except that the latter has a plumper, more rounded body. The spots on the forewings of the female are slightly larger than on the male, but this is only evident from close scrutiny. However, the female has a diminished extra spot in the suffused orange patches on the hindwings; this spot is absent in the male.

Females lay their eggs on the foodplant soon after emergence, and the larvae hatch after about 15 days, depending on the temperature. The larvae hibernate when partly grown, and resume feeding in the spring. Only one brood is produced each season.

The caterpillar is a stubby little creature with a tapered tail, and two thin dark stripes run down each side of its body. The basic colour is a pale brownish grey, and below the lower stripe is a small black dot on each segment.

When ready, the larva moves to the base of the foodplant and constructs a flimsy cocoon, pupating loose inside, in an upright position. The chrysalis is nut-brown in colour with pale wing cases, and a finely pointed tail.

Speckled Wood

Pararge aegeria Linnaeus

DISTRIBUTION: Europe through Asia Minor, Syria to Central Asia.

FOODPLANTS: Coarse grasses are selected by this species. Captive-bred larvae do particularly well on Cocksfoot (*Dactylis glomerata*).

GENERAL NOTES

The Speckled Wood is highly recommended to the beginner who is about to start breeding butterflies. It is very common in Britain throughout England, Wales and Ireland, with a few isolated colonies in Scotland. It is always a joy to see in woodland rides and clearings, basking on leaves where broken sunlight filters through the trees.

When alighting, this butterfly often makes short, rapid movements like those of a ballet dancer, quickly shifting its position.

The Speckled Wood has two broods, and the adults can first be seen in April and May. Later emerging females lay their eggs over a much longer period of time, and the second-brood adults which emerge as a result continue to appear for over two months, extending the flying period well into September.

The female is slightly larger than the male, and paler in colour. She is also better marked, with large white patterns on the forewings, and around the eye-spots on the hindwings.

Females lay their white eggs on the stems and blades of coarser grasses, soon after emergence, and the caterpillars take about three weeks to mature. The larva is white at first with a conspicuously black head, but after the first of four instars, it turns green. The caterpillars lie along the blades of grass, feeding from the tip, or stripping one side of the blade. At this stage they are very difficult to see, and it is much easier to capture a female to begin a captive breeding colony.

At maturity, the larvae hang from the tail, often in tussocks of grass, to pupate. The chrysalis is light greyish brown, and has a stubby appearance. As the weather grows colder, some of the larvae pupate and remain dormant for the winter. Others crawl into tussocks of grass where they remain in a state of semi-hibernation, and will continue to feed occasionally in the winter, on particularly warm days. The Speckled Wood is the only British species that will overwinter in two phases of its life cycle.

Wall Brown

Lasiommata megera Linnaeus

DISTRIBUTION: Europe through Asia Minor to Syria, Lebanon, Iran, north Africa.

FOODPLANTS: Any species of coarser grasses. Cocksfoot (*Dactylis glomerata*) is probably favoured most.

GENERAL NOTES

In Britain the Wall Brown is widespread throughout England, Wales and Ireland, and occurs as far north as southern Scotland. Although closely related to the Speckled Wood (*Pararge aegeria*), it prefers a much hotter environment. The butterflies search out large stone surfaces on sunlit grassy banks, and bask fully exposed in the summer heat. Favourite haunts are old quarries, and banks of disused railway track, especially where earth has been eroded to expose bare stone. The Wall Brown will also frequent country roadside verges and lanes, where the previous year's grasses are laid flat, and catch the scorching sun's rays.

The flight of these butterflies is swift and strong, uncharacteristic of the Satyrids. Like the Speckled Wood, they will flash their wings when alighting, repeatedly shifting position before starting to feed.

The female is larger than the male, and slightly paler in colour. The male has a small spot on the underside of the forewing, towards the wingtip, adjacent to the eye-spot. This is absent in the female.

The butterflies are first seen out in May, taking nectar from spring flowers. The females lay pale green eggs on the stems and blades of coarse grasses. The caterpillars grow rapidly, pupating in three to four weeks depending on temperature.

The pupae are larger than those of the Speckled Wood, and very dark (almost black) in colour; they also have a row of small white spots each side of the abdominal section. The pupa hangs from a silken pad by the cremaster.

Two or occasionally three broods are produced each season, and they overwinter as partly grown larvae. On warm days during hibernation, the caterpillars will venture out to feed, returning to shelter in tussocks of grass.

Small Heath

Coenonympha pamphilus Linnaeus

DISTRIBUTION: Europe, Asia Minor to Iran, Iraq, north Africa.

FOODPLANTS: Annual Meadow Grass (*Poa annua*) and any of the small-bladed grasses.

GENERAL NOTES

The Small Heath is a very common species throughout Britain and Ireland and is widely distributed. It can often be seen in very large numbers, settled on the ground, regardless of the terrain. These butterflies will fly in sunny or cloudy weather, providing it is warm, fluttering from underfoot when disturbed. Although the Small Heath frequents open ground, it prefers areas which offer some shelter from the wind, especially if ground cover is sparse. Short grasses, with open patches containing thistles and other grassland flowers, provide an ideal habitat.

The adults appear towards the end of May, and eggs are laid on short grasses. The Small Heath is double-brooded in the southern counties, but only single-brooded further north. Where they are single-brooded, the larvae can take up to 10 months to mature, overwintering in a state of semi-hibernation.

Adults of the second brood emerge much later in the following season, extending the flying period from May to September.

Both egg and larva are green, the caterpillar resembling the Speckled Wood, but it is much smaller and striped in various shades of green. The pupa is also green, and hangs by the tail, attached to a pad of silk amongst the grasses.

Large Heath

Coenonympha tullia Müller

DISTRIBUTION: North and central Europe across temperate Asia to the Pacific.

FOODPLANTS: Beaked Rush (*Rhynchospora alba*) is the wild foodplant, but captive-bred larvae will accept other grasses.

GENERAL NOTES

There are three geographical subspecies of the Large Heath, namely the Northern, Central and Southern. To make identification less complicated, only the markings on the underside of the wings of each subspecies are described.

The NORTHERN form, ssp. *scotica* Staudinger, is paler in colour than the other subspecies and therefore much easier to recognize. Both male and female have one small spot on the forewings, but the female also has two very diminished spots on the hindwings. All other markings are pale and slightly suffused.

The CENTRAL form, ssp. *polydama* Haworth, is considerably darker. The male has one spot on the forewings and six clearly defined spots on the hindwings. The female has three spots on the forewings, and six on the hindwings, but these are not as clearly defined as on the male. All other markings are clear and sharp.

The SOUTHERN form, ssp. *davus* Fabricius, is the darkest race, almost melanic in colour. The male has three spots on the forewings, and seven on the hindwings. The female has five spots on the forewings, and seven on the hindwings.

Of the three species, the last is the most impressive, both in colour and sharpness of detail. In all three, the females are slightly larger than the males, and also a little paler. Ssp. *scotica* females appear almost to be albinistic.

Although the subspecies are divided into British geographical regions ranging from north Wales to northern Scotland, it is possible to find any of them anywhere in the British distribution range. Generally, one can expect to find them more abundant in the localities given above.

The Large Heath frequents marshy hillsides and damp areas, to a height of approximately 600m (2,000ft). There is only one brood each season which emerges towards the end of June. The adults are short-lived, disappearing by the end of July.

Females lay their eggs singly on the foodplant, and the larvae hatch within about 15 days. After a few weeks, they go into hibernation, and resume feeding in March or April, depending on the geographical location, being later in the north.

The caterpillar is dark green in colour with two white stripes each side of the body running from head to tail. Between the two stripes is a slightly darker stripe.

When mature, the larvae pupate, hanging from the tail amongst grasses. The chrysalis is green, a little paler than the larva, and has sharp black streaking on the pupal wing cases.

Gatekeeper

Pyronia tithonus Linnaeus

DISTRIBUTION: Europe to Caucasus.

FOODPLANTS: Most species of coarser grasses.

GENERAL NOTES

The Gatekeeper is widespread in Britain throughout England and Wales, except in the far north. A few isolated colonies are reported in Ireland, but there are no confirmed reports of it in Scotland.

On a sunny day, Gatekeepers can often be seen in their hundreds on flowering bramble, especially in southern coastal areas. Although still common further north, they are found in much smaller numbers. Country lanes with short hedges are favourite haunts, and several individuals will often congregate in a sheltered gateway, hence this butterfly's most common name. It is also known as the Hedge Brown and the Small Meadow Brown. However, *P. tithonus* is easily distinguished from the Meadow Brown by size, as it is much smaller.

63

The adults are first seen on the wing in early July, several weeks later than the Meadow Brown. The female is larger than the male, and fatter bodied. The basic colour of the butterfly is brown, but the forewings are flushed in bright orange, leaving a broad border extending round the outer margins. In the orange towards the wingtip is a double-eyed spot. The hindwings have an orange flush towards the centre.

The males are slightly brighter in colour, but the orange on the forewing is broken by a bar of dark scent scales.

Eggs are laid singly on grasses soon after the butterflies appear, and only one brood is produced each season. The larvae are straw-coloured with dark stripes of varied thickness down the length of the body; they overwinter as quite small caterpillars, moving into tussocks of grass.

In the spring, the larvae resume feeding until maturity, finally pupating in June. The pupa is pale brown and darker towards the tail, and the pupal wing cases have darker brown streaks with similar markings down the abdominal section. The method of pupation is suspensi, hanging from the tail amongst the grasses.

Meadow Brown

Maniola jurtina Linnaeus

DISTRIBUTION: Europe, Canary Isles, North Africa, Asia Minor to Iran.

FOODPLANTS: Most species of grass suit this abundant species.

GENERAL NOTES

The Meadow Brown population can reach amazing proportions in the British Isles in the southern counties of England, and they are extremely common throughout the rest of Britain and Ireland. They can be seen in practically any grassland during July and August.

The adults begin to emerge in June, and eggs are laid in the grasses. The species is usually only single-brooded, but

The Peacock butterfly (*Inachis io*). Eggs are laid in batches on the underside of stinging nettle leaves. Young leaves are preferable.

Glanville Fritillary (*Melitaea cinxia*) caterpillars are gregarious for all their long larval period of some 10 months.

The moth-like Large Skipper (*Ochlodes venata*) enjoys feeding and basking on flower heads of thistle.

The female Marbled White (*Melanargia galathea*) is one of the few butterflies that lay its eggs at random, often while on the wing.

The Orange Tip (*Anthocharis cardamines*) is very difficult to spot when at rest and its caterpillars are cannibalistic.

The Small Tortoiseshell (*Aglais urticae*) is a highly successful and very widely distributed species.

Red Admiral butterflies (*Vanessa atalanta*) have strong migratory instincts. Caterpillars hide away in tent-like constructions amongst the leaves of their foodplants.

The freshly emerged male *Papilio aegeus aegeus* (top left) dries his wings in preparation of his search for a partner.

The huge *Troides* butterflies, Golden Birdwings (bottom left), are found in much of South East Asia from Sri Lanka and India to Papua New Guinea.

Female *Papilio aegeus aegeus* (above) from Australia behaves as if it could have been designed for captive breeding.

Cressida cressida (above) from Australia is often known as Old Greasy.

This close-up shot of *Papilio machaon* (left) shows its huge compound eyes.

Papilio memnon (below). This beautiful species, which is not always tailed, is a *Citrus* feeder and does particularly well when fed on skimmia.

Papilio demoleus is a popular *Citrus* feeder bred in large numbers at butterfly exhibitions.

European Swallowtail butterflies (*Papilio machaon*) are a great favourite amongst young enthusiasts, who often use carrot as a substitute foodplant.

The colourful female of *Hypolimnas bolina* (above) from Australia. Caterpillars take readily to stinging nettle.

The Owl butterfly (*Caligo brasiliensis*) (left) moves into the shade of trees as the sun gets hotter. They fly in the early morning and again in the evening.

Zerinthia polyxena, the European Map butterfly, is a strikingly marked species. Its foodplant is *Aristolochia*.

Scolitantides orion. This pretty Lycaenid butterfly occurs in Spain, central France to central Asia and Japan.

Danaus chrisippus is a close relative of the famous Monarch or Milkweed – *Danaus plexippus.*

A freshly emerged *Heliconius melpomone* (above)
gathers strength resting on a lantana leaf.

Some species of Heliconid, such as these
Heliconius erato (below), often return to the same
roosting perch throughout their long lives.

An example (above) of the strange markings that occur in *Heliconius melpomone* (var. *croxstonii*).

Heliconius melpomone (below) can be seen digesting pollen, which helps this family live a long, active life.

This large African mantis female wanders in search of prey.

These are the first scorpions bred by myself and John Midwinter in 1972 at Bourton-on-the-Water, England.

The bizarre head of the popular stick insect *Extatosoma tiaratum* which is found in northern Australia and throughout Papua New Guinea.

In its natural habitat the leaf insect (*Phyllium crucifolium*) of Java must be very hard to spot.

If a leaf insect loses a leg at first instar it will be replaced more or less intact. After this it will only be partially replaced, as with this specimen.

The Malayan Jungle Nymph (*Heteropteryx dilatata*) is a recent addition to the ever-increasing list of species of Phasmid to be bred as pets by the enthusiast.

The Malayan Jungle Nymph must be one of the most striking species of stick insect in the world.

The Mexican Red Rump (*Brachypelma vagans*) (right). I once lost one to a cricket during a moult.

Every spider keeper wants the Rusty-kneed Tarantula (*Brachypelma smithi*) (below) and this has been one of the foremost reasons for the rapid decline of numbers in the wild.

Acromyrmex octospinosus (left) seen here cutting a rose leaf. One side of the mandible is dug into the leaf and the other is drawn towards it, slowly slicing through.

Seen below is a small part of a fungus garden containing thousands of ants. *Acromyrmex octospinosus* was my first colony which lasted over 10 years.

occasionally hot seasons result in a second brood in September. The second-brood caterpillars join some of the first brood which are slow-growing, progressing through six instars as they mature.

The appearance of the larvae is typical of the grass feeders, being fleshy bodied with a tapered tail. The underside of the caterpillar is dark green, the topside pale green. There is a distinct edge to the two colours just above the prolegs, and they are covered in fine white hairs.

Hibernation is only partial, as the larvae will spasmodically feed, except in very cold spells, when they remain dormant and low to the ground. Some of the larvae can be nearly 10 months old when they finally pupate, and the pupa hangs from the tail by the cremaster.

The chrysalis is grass-green in colour, with a few much darker green markings. Its colour and texture make it very difficult to find.

Ringlet

Aphantopus hyperantus Linnaeus

DISTRIBUTION: Europe to Korea.

FOODPLANTS: Most coarse grasses.

GENERAL NOTES

In the British Isles the Ringlet is well distributed in England and Wales, and locally in southern Scotland and it is common throughout Ireland.

These butterflies can often be seen sharing their habitat with the Meadow Brown and Speckled Wood. They feed from woodland flowers and often favour damper situations. They frequent woodland clearings and rides, sunny roadside verges and hedgerows. This type of habitat ensures that the eggs are never far from the larval foodplant.

The male is velvet black on the upperside, and a little paler underneath. Seven spots on the underside are ringed in a dull yellow, making them sharp and well defined. The female is slightly larger and paler, with an extra spot on the forewing.

65

When sunlight catches the wings at certain angles, they assume a golden hue.

The Ringlet is out towards the end of June, and remains on the wing until around mid-August. Only one brood is produced, and most of their life is spent as larvae, taking about nine months to mature.

Females begin laying their pale green eggs soon after emergence, and the Ringlet is one of the few species which will drop eggs whilst in flight. They will also lay while walking amongst the grasses.

The eggs hatch after about two weeks, and the caterpillars begin their slow progress through five instars. They keep low to the ground during the day, feeding at night from coarse grasses. The larva is a pale brownish colour, well camouflaged amongst degenerated grasses near the ground. Its skin texture is smooth, and a grey and dark brown stripe runs down each side of its body. The larva is also covered in very short, fine hairs.

The caterpillars do not go completely into hibernation, and will become active enough to feed on warmer days. However, they resume regular feeding in the spring and attain full growth towards the end of May.

For pupation, the larvae construct a flimsy shelter at the base of the foodplant, using fine grasses drawn together with silk. They then pupate inside, involuti. The pupa is the same colour as the larva, with pale pupal wing cases.

Marbled White
Melanargia galathea Linnaeus

DISTRIBUTION: Europe through southern Russia to Iran.

FOODPLANTS: Cocksfoot (*Dactylis glomerata*) and many other species of grasses.

GENERAL NOTES
In Britain this single-brooded species does not occur in Ireland or Scotland, but is common from the Cotswolds down to the southern counties of England. There are also a few

colonies in south Wales and in Yorkshire.

Open sections of disused railway track are often favoured, as well as overgrown, sunlit quarries, and scrubby meadowland which is never ploughed. Several can often be found adorning a thistle-head or other grassland flower. In flight, the butterfly seems larger than it really is, but its marbled wings make identification easy. The adults will fly in sunny or cloudy weather, provided that the air is reasonably warm.

The Marbled White is a colonial species, often seen in large numbers, and they appear to prefer specific locations in a habitat that would seem generally unvarying. They occur year after year in the same place, but a stray individual may be seen on occasion, dancing along a hedgerow.

Although a common species where it occurs, the Marbled White is seldom seen or recognized by the general public. The female is a little larger than the male, and the underside has a dull yellowish tinge. This also occurs in the male to a lesser degree, but he is brighter, and the marbled black and white is sharper.

Like the Ringlet, the females lay their eggs whilst on the wing; these are the only two British species which do this. The white eggs produce straw-coloured larvae which later turn green, faintly striped in yellow down each side. In the early stages, they rest on dead grasses, making discovery by predators very difficult.

The larvae take little or no food prior to hibernation, but begin to feed very early in the year, when many other species are still dormant. When ready, the caterpillar makes its way to the base of the foodplant, and pupates loose, beneath blades of grass held together by a few strands of silk. The chrysalis is a creamy colour, tinged with golden brown, and the butterflies emerge about three weeks later.

Grayling

Hipparchia semele Linnaeus

DISTRIBUTION: Europe to southern Russia.

FOODPLANTS: Most species of coarse grass.

GENERAL NOTES

Distribution of the various subspecies of Grayling in Britain is given below, but generally, these butterflies are more common in warmer, southern latitudes. There are six geographical subspecies, all of which deserve mention. The English form is ssp. *anglorum* Verity. Ssp. *thyone* Thompson is found on the Great Orme's Head in north Wales, and is slightly smaller than the others, with a duller coloration. Eastern Scotland is the home of ssp. *scota* Verity, which is brighter and more orange. The Inner Hebrides form, ssp. *atlantica* Harrison, is even brighter, especially the female. The Irish form, ssp. *hibernica* Howarth, can be found in many coastal locations, and is also bright and sharply marked. In Clare and Galway, the duller ssp. *clarensis* de Lattin can be found, but this form is not so common, particularly in Galway. In general, the female is larger, better marked and much brighter than the male.

The Grayling prefers a habitat offering shelter and sunlight, rarely flying on dull days. Like the Small Heath, they frequent areas where ground cover is sparse, with open patches of soil and rocky ground to bask on in the full sunshine. They always rest with wings closed, turning to face the sun, and therefore cast no shadow. Scrubby hillsides near the coast are likely places to find them.

Butterflies are seen from mid-July until September, and the females lay singly on the foodplant. The caterpillars begin to appear in early August. Larvae hibernate when about half-grown.

The mature larvae is straw-coloured, and quite heavily striped in dark grey which can be almost black. They progress through five instars, taking over 10 months to attain full growth, before finally pupating in June. The method of pupation is unique to a butterfly, and more reminiscent of a moth. The larva burrows just under the ground surface, constructs a flimsy cocoon to create a small cavity, and pupates inside, upside down. The chrysalis is brown, quite rich in colour, and the pupal wing cases are slightly paler.

NYMPHALIDAE:
Brush-footed

These butterflies cannot use their first pair, or prothoracic, legs for walking, as they are reduced and without claws. Those of the male are covered with brush-like hairs, but the female's are spiny at the tips. Close examination of a Nymphalid whilst feeding will reveal that these under-developed legs are held tight against the thorax, and are only lowered when tasting leaves for egg-laying or feeding.

This family contains five subfamilies: Limenitinae (White Admiral), Vanessinae (Red Admiral, Peacock and Comma), Apaturinae (Purple Emperor), Argynninae (the large Fritillaries), and Melitaeinae (the smaller Fritillaries).

This is one of the largest families, containing several thousand species worldwide, and amongst these are the most colourful and also the most powerful butterflies. For striking colours, we immediately think of the Red Admiral or the Peacock, but looking through a book on exotic butterflies, the *Agrias*, *Callithea*, *Cethosia* and *Prepona* genera are just a few which exhibit breathtaking colour and variable form.

Some are habitual wanderers, able to travel great distances, limited only by the distribution of foodplant or temperature.

The larvae are usually spiny, and the skin often contains distasteful or poisonous chemicals, such as cyanide. Most birds find them repugnant, one of the few exceptions being the cuckoo, which will take Peacock and Small Tortoiseshell larvae, bursting the body of the larva and running it through the beak to disgorge the contents before discarding the skin.

The Red Admiral and Painted Lady are migrants, which appear in Britain in the spring from Europe and Africa. Both produce home-bred butterflies each season, but are unable to withstand the long, wet winter months.

The Small Tortoiseshell and Peacock can often be found

Some caterpillars have poisonous spines to protect them from predators. Seen here as an example is *Hypolimnas bolina* from Australia.

hibernating in Britain in garden sheds, houses and farm buildings, whereas the Comma always chooses a wilder situation: hollow trees, or even in the rough bark of an oak or elm. The Vanessids are regular visitors to garden flowers in both town and country, making a familiar splash of colour on buddleia or sedum.

The larger Fritillaries are not as gaudy and much less familiar than the Vanessids, but they have all the qualities associated with their race. Dark Green, High Brown and

Silver-washed Fritillaries are able to battle against strong winds, and fly effortlessly for miles. However, they are never seen in towns and cities, keeping to rough scrubland, open ground and marginal woodland.

The smaller Fritillaries are somewhat uncharacteristic of Nymphalids, being localized and weak in flight compared with their relatives.

Our most impressive species must be the Purple Emperor: few people have seen one alive, but its majestic flight and iridescent colours are sight to be remembered.

Red Admiral

Vanessa atalanta Linnaeus

DISTRIBUTION: Europe, north Africa, Asia Minor, Palestine, Himalayas to central Asia, throughout North America to Guatemala and Haiti.

FOODPLANTS: Stinging Nettle (*Urtica dioica*) is the principal foodplant, but Hops (*Humulus lupulus*) are also reported to be taken.

GENERAL NOTES

This lovely butterfly has a strong flight, and can be seen virtually anywhere in the British Isles. It is a familiar sight in parks, gardens and other open situations, and enjoys basking in full sunlight on open patches of soil, warm stone walls or sheltered trees. They are attracted to garden flowers, particularly buddleia or sedum, and, if disturbed, will circle and return quickly to continue feeding. At harvest time, many will congregate in fruit orchards to feed on fallen plums or damsons, regularly joined by the Comma which also enjoys the same diet.

Red Admirals usually arrive in Britain in May, migrating from the Continent. Their first home broods appear in July, and are slightly larger than their parents. They have deep velvet black and brilliant red markings, and are very beautiful. Eggs are laid singly on the upper surface of nettle leaves, unlike Peacocks and Small Tortoiseshells which lay in large batches. The larvae vary in colour from pale grey to almost black, and are covered with long bristled spines. They have five yellowish crescents which cross the segmental divisions, running down each side, and these start from the sixth segment.

The caterpillar draws a leaf together with silk to make a tent, concealing itself inside, but, despite this solitary hiding place, their numbers are greatly reduced by parasitic wasps. The chrysalis hangs by the tail in the undergrowth, usually away from the foodplant. Although many adults attempt to overwinter, few if any survive. It is thought that British-bred butterflies may migrate to France and Spain.

Painted Lady
Vanessa cardui Linnaeus

DISTRIBUTION: Whole world except north and south polar ice caps and South America.

FOODPLANTS: Spear Thistle (*Cirsium vulgare*) is one of the many species of thistle used. Other foodplants are reported, including Viper's Bugloss (*Echium vulgare*), Burdock (*Arctium*), Mallow (*Malva*), and Stinging Nettle (*Urtica dioica*). I have always used nettle for captive breeding.

GENERAL NOTES

In warmer climates, the Painted Lady is a continuously brooded species, and as a migrant can turn up almost anywhere in Britain. However, they are much less common than the Red Admiral, and their numbers fluctuate from year to year. The powerful, and swift-flying butterflies arrive in this country to breed from May onwards. Buddleia is one of their favourite flowers, and will often attract them in large numbers.

They spend long periods basking in the sunshine, preferring open patches of soil, and if disturbed will fly off at high speed, returning to settle again in almost the same spot.

Females lay their eggs on thistle leaves towards the end of May, or in June, and the larva draws a leaf together with silk, leaving fine strands stretching like gossamer across the foodplant. Thistle has thick, fleshy leaves, and this enables the caterpillar to feed from the inside of its shelter without causing perforations. When one food source is exhausted, it moves on, making another shelter.

At maturity, the larva is almost black with reddish prolegs. It has a broken yellow lateral line down each side, and is sparsely covered in bristled spines. In the final instar, the larva feeds in the open, finally pupating on the foodplant hanging from the cremaster, inside a leaf shelter.

The adults emerge after about 10 days, and a second and occasionally a third brood are produced in good seasons. As the winter approaches, they fly south from Britain, some migrating across the English Channel. Many die, however, as they are unable to hibernate. Home-bred specimens are larger and brighter than the migrants. Greater temperature fluctuation often makes markings more variable with larger marginal spotting.

White Admiral

Ladoga (Limenitis) camilla Linnaeus

DISTRIBUTION: West and central Europe across Russia and central Asia to China and Japan.

FOODPLANTS: Wild Honeysuckle (*Lonicera periclymenum*) is the only foodplant.

GENERAL NOTES

White Admirals are most common in England in the southeast and in the New Forest, but localized colonies can be found in the Midlands and throughout the southern counties.

The butterflies are out in July, and their graceful gliding flight can be seen in woodland and forest clearings for only two to three weeks. Their main food source is nectar from the flowers of blackberry bramble; when they are gone, the butterflies soon die.

Females deposit eggs on the leaf edges of wild honeysuckle, and they hatch towards the end of the month.

73

The caterpillar spins a cocoon-like tube, interwoven with its droppings, and conceals itself inside, appearing to be an extension of the central rib of a leaf. The second to the fifth segments are slightly thickened, and the second, fourth and fifth segments carry two long, bristled spines. The remaining segments each carry two smaller spines, and the body is bright green.

The larvae feed mostly at night, to the right and left of the leaf tip, returning to the shelter of the tube by day. With the approach of winter, the caterpillar prepares for hibernation, by constructing a capsule to protect and conceal it through the winter. To achieve this, it wraps what remains of its leaf around itself, and secures it with silk.

Honeysuckle is deciduous; the larvae have to prevent the leaves from falling, and do so by spinning silk around the leaf stem and petiole, anchoring it firmly to the vine. The best time to collect breeding stock is after the leaves have fallen, as the hibernaculum remains on the vine, and is easy to spot.

In the spring, the larvae continue to feed, pupating in June. The chrysalis, which hangs by the cremaster, is quite exceptional in its dorsal projection and extended wing cases, combined with its unusual coloration.

Purple Emperor

Apatura iris Linnaeus

DISTRIBUTION: West Europe to Asia Minor.

FOODPLANT: Broad-leaved Sallow (*Salix caprea*).

GENERAL NOTES

Found in southern central England, the Purple Emperor is a single-brooded species, and is on the wing for most of July and August. It seems to require a specific type of habitat to be successful.

Although the foodplant is sallow, the presence of mature oak trees is evidently essential, and the butterflies spend most of their time flying and sunning themselves in the canopy of these trees.

Flowers rarely attract the Purple Emperor; they prefer to suck the juices of carrion, dung or tree sap. A partly decomposed rabbit would make good bait, if trying to entice one of these splendid butterflies to the ground. The Purple Emperor is the only British butterfly to have iridescent colouring on its wings, which is caused by light refraction. The only time one would see both sides of its wings blue is if they were spread flat. To see this powerful butterfly flashing blue in bright sunshine is a very memorable experience.

Eggs are laid singly on the upper surface of leaves, in July. The larvae are green and almost the same colour and texture as the foodplant. In the winter, they hibernate at the third instar, turning brown to match the colour of sallow bark. When feeding recommences in the spring, they turn green once more.

Interesting features of these caterpillars are the two long, pointed horns forming a 'V' at the head, and the tail tapers to a fine point.

Pupation takes place in June, and the chrysalis hangs by the tail. Even this stage is quite spectacular: the pupa has a flattened form, which has a rounded edge, looking so much like a sallow leaf that it is virtually impossible to discover.

Small Tortoiseshell

Aglais urticae Linnaeus

DISTRIBUTION: Europe through northern Asia to Soviet–Chinese border.

FOODPLANT: Stinging Nettle (*Urtica dioica*) is the only known foodplant.

GENERAL NOTES

The Small Tortoiseshell is one of the commonest British butterflies, and can be found throughout the British Isles. A bed of sedum or a buddleia will attract them in their hundreds, and they are a well-loved and familiar sight in cities or country villages alike.

Two and, occasionally, three broods are produced between

May and August, and females lay batches of up to 150 eggs on the underside of nettle leaves. They prefer young, terminal growth to lay on, selecting open situations with great care. In a long stretch of nettle, females will lay where there is an indentation in the ground, offering a little extra protection, or in the sheltered corner of a field. Cutting nettle down in late May will force it to produce tender new growth, and this may attract the later broods.

The larvae are greyish black with white flecking down the sides and back, and they have several bristled spines to each segment. They feed in large clusters until the final instar, cocooning themselves in silken shelters for protection. When one food source is exhausted, they move to the next, spinning another shelter.

During the final instar, the larvae separate into ones and twos, keeping to the underside of the leaves. At full growth, they move away from the foodplant to seek out a safe and sheltered pupation site, and here they hang by the tail from a silken pad. Millions are killed by parasitic wasps which emerge from the dead pupal case.

The pupae vary in colour: some are brown, and others have a greenish tinge. They emerge after about 10 days. Butterflies of the autumn brood are sexually immature, remaining so through hibernation. They are on the wing in early March, as soon as it is warm enough, feeding from spring flowers and pussy willow.

Large Tortoiseshell
Nymphalis polychloros Linneaus

DISTRIBUTION: Europe to Asia and Himalayas.

FOODPLANTS: The principal foodplant is Elm (*Ulmus*), but they will also take Sallow and Willow (*Salix*). Various fruit trees are also reported.

GENERAL NOTES

This butterfly is the largest of the British Vanessids, and also the rarest. Although it is a resident species, some butterflies do occasionally appear as migrants.

Spasmodic sightings of the Large Tortoiseshell seem to indicate that regular colonization in any one area is unusual. This fact alone would suggest that any increase in its numbers is unlikely. The destruction of millions of elm trees by Dutch Elm Disease would make it difficult for a roving female to find suitable laying sites, and so its position is even more precarious. I have only ever seen one Large Tortoiseshell in the wild: this was on a disused railway track near Andoversford in Gloucestershire, in June 1973.

Large Tortoiseshells spend long periods basking in the sun, and seldom visit flowers, preferring tree sap or soft fruit. The species is single-brooded, producing eggs in April after a long hibernation.

On finding a site, usually high in an elm tree, the female lays a band of eggs encircling a twig. The caterpillars stay together, feeding in large clusters, stripping leaves in ever-increasing quantities as they progress through five instars. They are typical Vanessid caterpillars, similar to the Peacock and Small Tortoiseshell, but attain a larger size, and their spiky hairs have a brownish tint. By June, they are ready to pupate, but first descend to the ground in search of a secluded hiding place. The pupa hangs from a silken pad, and emerges after about 15 days, depending on temperature.

Large Tortoiseshells begin hibernation very early, often towards the end of July, and take little or no nourishment prior to their winter sleep. They remain dormant for almost nine months, venturing out again in April.

Peacock

Inachis io Linnaeus

DISTRIBUTION: Europe, eastwards through Asia to Japan.

FOODPLANT: Stinging Nettle (*Urtica dioica*) is the only foodplant.

GENERAL NOTES

In Britain these striking butterflies range over the whole of England, extending into southern Scotland. Though they are very prone to the unwanted attentions of parasitic wasps, Peacock butterflies continue to flourish.

The blue flowers of scabious and those of various thistles are often visited by this butterfly, but once again buddleia is much preferred. They tend to be territorial, and have favourite sites for basking. If disturbed, they will return quickly to exactly the same position, even turning, once settled, to face in the same direction. If another butterfly comes too near, it is immediately investigated and often chased away.

In May, the females lay large, solid batches of eggs on the underside of stinging nettle leaves. The larvae, like those of the Small Tortoiseshell, feed gregariously until the final instar.

Although it is perhaps a little difficult in the early stages, the caterpillars are easily distinguishable from the Small Tortoiseshell, being larger, and jet black in colour. They also have a smattering of pure white spots.

Peacock caterpillars produce quite a sizeable silken tent to feed under, and leave a trail of destruction through the nettle patch, which is easily spotted by the enthusiast.

In the final instar, the caterpillars disperse and feed singly, pupating away from the foodplant and hanging by the tail. Captive breeding will produce at least two broods in a season, and, with higher temperatures, even three. In the wild, Peacocks are usually single-brooded.

Apart from the inevitable few stragglers, Peacocks tend to hibernate earlier than Small Tortoiseshells, and are often found sleeping communally.

Comma

Polygonia c-album Linnaeus

DISTRIBUTION: Europe to north Africa, central Asia to Soviet–Chinese border, Himalayas, North America (from

78

Saskatchewan River to east Colorado, south to the Mississippi and central Georgia).

FOODPLANTS: Stinging Nettle (*Urtica dioica*) is probably the principal foodplant, but larvae will also take Hops (*Humulus*), Sallow (*Salix*), Elm (*Ulmus*) and some soft fruit leaves.

GENERAL NOTES

Sixty-five years ago, the Comma was a rare and localized species in Britain. Today it is widespread from Shropshire to the southern counties, and happily it is still expanding its range. It has strong territorial tendencies, and, if disturbed, will persistently return to its resting place. They appear to be equally at home basking on open patches of soil and garden paths, or quite high on a leaf in full sunlight. During spring and summer, Commas can be seen feeding from a variety of wild and garden flowers. They are also a common sight feeding on fallen fruit in the company of Red Admirals and wasps.

This butterfly has the most unusual indented wing edges, quite different from any other British species. It spends long periods basking in the sun with its wings spread flat, and in this position the forewings are stretched so that a gap appears between the fore- and hindwings; this adds to the indented outline, giving it almost the appearance of a set specimen.

Eggs are laid singly or in very small batches, on the upper surface of leaves, soon after the butterflies venture from hibernation – which is towards the end of April. The first eggs produce a pale form of the species (form *hutchinsoni*); later eggs produce the normal, darker form. Form *hutchinsoni* produces the first of the second brood, and the new, darker form produces a prolonged, second brood which hibernates early.

Later in the autumn, butterflies of the second brood produced by the *hutchinsoni* also go into hibernation, increasing the numbers and forming the breeding stock for the following season.

The larvae are solitary, keeping to the underside of the

leaves, and feeding away from the edges, perforating them as they move about the foodplant. In later stages of development, the larvae have a brilliant white stripe running along the back, which is in complete contrast to the brown sides and underside.

The first broods pupate in June. At this stage, the larvae are most often found wandering away from the foodplant in search of a pupation site, where they hang by the tail.

Heath Fritillary
Mellicta athalia Rottemburg

DISTRIBUTION: Europe through temperate zone to Japan.

FOODPLANTS: Cow-wheat (*Melampyrum pratense*) is the main foodplant. The larvae will also take Foxglove (*Digitalis purpurea*), Wood Sage (*Teucrium scorodonia*), and Ribwort (*Plantago lanceolata*). A number of other plants are also reported, including some garden plants.

GENERAL NOTES
In England strong colonies of this species can be found in Devon and Cornwall, where the habitat is suitable. There are also a few very local colonies in Kent. Several foodplants of this species grow on the fringes of small groups of trees, where they are protected from wind. This type of location, therefore, is likely to be favoured by the Heath Fritillary. Woodland clearings, where trees have been thinned, are a suitable breeding ground.

The females are a little larger than the males, and their coloration is somewhat softer. The butterflies enjoy basking in the sunshine with wings spread flat, and several individuals are usually seen together. If disturbed, their flight is weak, almost as if it is their maiden flight, and they soon settle again once out of reach.

The females lay about 300 eggs towards the end of June, in several batches on the chosen foodplant. The larvae live beneath the leaves in masses of about 80, protected by a loose silken web. The larvae are small, slow-moving and dumpy, typical of the smaller Fritillaries, and covered in short, orange spiky hairs laid out in rows across each segment. When not quite half-grown, the larvae hibernate, low down on the foodplant, under the protection of a silken web. In spring, they resume feeding, and progress through the remainder of seven instars. The caterpillars prefer to feed on warm, sunny days; in cooler, cloudy weather they are sluggish, hiding away amongst the leaves of the foodplant.

Pupation takes place in June, and the pupae hang from grass stems or other suitable support by the tail. The butterflies emerge after about two weeks, depending on temperature, and are on the wing for about five to six weeks.

Glanville Fritillary
Melitaea cinxia Linnaeus

DISTRIBUTION: Europe to Soviet–Chinese border, Morocco.

FOODPLANTS: Sea Plantain (*Plantago maritima*) and Ribwort (*Plantago lanceolata*).

GENERAL NOTES

For just one month of the year, this small butterfly is on the wing in Britain, but only on the Isle of Wight. This is the sole breeding location in the British Isles where it lives under cliffs and in rough ground.

Although similar in appearance to the Heath Fritillary, the Glanville Fritillary is darker and sharper. It also has a row of spots on the hindwings between the central and outer margin. These spots are absent on the Heath Fritillary. There is also a marked difference between male and female, the latter being larger, with rounded wings.

The butterflies emerge in the middle of May, and produce eggs shortly afterwards. The eggs are laid in a mass on the leaves of the foodplant.

On hatching, the larvae feed gregariously, consuming whole plants from the protection of a communal web. As one plant is eaten, they move to a fresh one and spin another web. As winter approaches, the caterpillars congregate at the base of the foodplant, and hibernate there, still under the protection of a silken web.

In the spring, they continue to feed, but out in the open, and progress through seven instars before finally dispersing to pupate, hanging from the tail.

Pearl-bordered Fritillary

Boloria (Clossiana) euphrosyne Linnaeus

DISTRIBUTION: West and central Europe through northern and central Asia to Korea, North America.

FOODPLANTS: Dog Violet (*Viola canina*) and other species of violets.

GENERAL NOTES
The Pearl-bordered Fritillary is widely distributed in the British Isles throughout England and Wales. Although quite common in Scotland, it is much scarcer in Ireland. However, it is most prolific in the southern counties of England, and the Cotswolds. The butterflies frequent marginal woodland, and forest rides and clearings.

These butterflies are quite difficult to distinguish from the Small Pearl-bordered Fritillary (see below). However, *B. selene* is a little paler on the upperside, looking less sharp, and the two lines of marking on the outer margins of the wings merge into one, giving the appearance of pale spots. This is absent in *B. euphrosyne*. On the underside of *B. selene*, particularly on the hindwings, the markings on the outer margin are outlined in black, giving a clearer, sharper look. The 'silver plating' on the inner margins is more extensive, spanning the hindwing. *B. selene* also has a row of sharp, black spots between the inner and outer margin on the hindwings; again, this is absent in *B. euphrosyne*.

The adults are first seen on the wing in early May, three or four weeks earlier than *B. selene*. Females lay their eggs on violet leaves, and the larvae hatch within seven or eight days, depending on temperature. In good seasons, an occasional second brood has been found in August, but usually the larvae only feed for a short time before going into early hibernation, even though the best of the summer weather is still to come.

The caterpillars of the Pearl-bordered Fritillary are black, spined and flecked with white, while those of *B. selene* are quite different being brown with two bristle horns just behind the head.

The larvae commence serious feeding in the spring, growing through five instars and pupating towards the end of April or early May. The pupae hang from the tail in the undergrowth, emerging within about two weeks.

Small Pearl-bordered Fritillary
Boloria (Clossiana) selene Denis and Schiffermüller

DISTRIBUTION: West and central Europe, northern and central Asia to Korea, North America (Alaska, east to New England).

FOODPLANTS: Dog Violet (*Viola canina*) is the principal foodplant, but most other violet species are taken.

GENERAL NOTES

The Small Pearl-bordered Fritillary is widespread over the whole of Britain, with the exception of some eastern regions, but they are most common in the southern counties and on the grassland slopes of central Wales. This species does not occur in Ireland. It is primarily a woodland species, but the butterflies often venture into meadowlands, frequently sharing their habitat with the Pearl-bordered Fritillary.

The features which distinguish this species from the Pearl-bordered Fritillary (see above) are described in the general notes for the latter. If specimens of each species are compared closely, the differences soon become apparent.

The Small Pearl-bordered Fritillary is on the wing in June, and eggs are laid singly on violet leaves. The larvae feed from the underside of the leaf until they are about half-grown, or a little less. At this stage, they go into hibernation, moving close to the ground amongst the degenerating leaves of the foodplant.

In the spring, feeding continues until May, and the pupae hang from the tail, emerging in June. Occasionally second broods occur in August and even September.

Dark Green Fritillary
Argynnis (Mesoacidalia) aglaja Linnaeus

DISTRIBUTION: Europe across Asia to China and Japan, Morocco.

FOODPLANTS: Dog Violet (*Viola canina*) is probably the principal foodplant, but any violet will be taken. Captive-bred larvae will take pansy.

GENERAL NOTES

The Dark Green Fritillary is a single-brooded species which is widely distributed throughout Britain. However, it is most common in the south. There are also a few occurrences in Ireland.

These butterflies are strong fliers, with apparent nomadic tendencies, often flying several miles without rest. They will take nectar from most suitable wild flowers, and occasionally visit a country garden. Their wings soon become battered and torn from flying through scrub and tall grasses. Strong winds which keep other species immobile do not deter the Dark Green Fritillary; they almost seem to enjoy them.

The females are noticeably larger than the males, darker in colour, and have rounded wings.

Adults are first seen in July, and the females lay their eggs on violet leaves. Once a location has been found, they may lay on any part of the plant, even on the ground nearby.

The eggs hatch after about three weeks, and the tiny larvae eat only their eggshells before going immediately into hibernation until the following March. By June, the larvae are fully grown, and very beautiful. Although typical Nymphalid larvae, very similar to the Peacock, they are a deep golden brown, with rust-coloured blotches down the side.

In early July, the caterpillar will draw several leaves loosely around itself, fastening them together with silk. It then pupates inside the structure, hanging by the tail.

High Brown Fritillary
Argynnis (Fabriciana) adippe Linnaeus

DISTRIBUTION: Europe, temperate Asia to north Africa.

FOODPLANTS: Dog Violet (*Viola canina*) is the primary foodplant, but captive-bred larvae will take any violet species.

GENERAL NOTES

This shy butterfly is a single-brooded species, and, although quite common, is seldom seen. In Britain it favours the southern counties of England, but can be found throughout England and Wales. The High Brown Fritillary is primarily a woodland species, but scrubland, grassy banks and old quarries are also favoured haunts.

It is difficult to distinguish this species from the Dark Green Fritillary, when viewing the topside of the wings, but it is much easier from the underside. The metallic silver spots on the High Brown Fritillary are somewhat larger, and it lacks the brushed green colour of the Dark Green Fritillary, having a reddish colour instead.

The butterflies are first seen on the wing in early July, and fly for about four to five weeks. When feeding or resting, they appear very striking and robust insects. They give the impression of being larger than they really are, and sunshine seems to bring a golden glow to their wings as they move swiftly through the air.

Mating and egg-laying take place in June, and the females will lay on any part of the violet foodplant, and on vegetation close by. The larvae form up inside the egg, and then remain dormant until the following March, before hatching.

As with the Dark Green Fritillary, the caterpillars are exceptional, being a rich, golden brown. However, the High Brown Fritillary larvae have longer spines and a sharp white line down the centre of the back.

Their pupation technique is the same as for the Dark Green Fritillary: the caterpillar will draw several leaves together with silk, and in this loose structure will hang by the cremaster.

Silver-washed Fritillary
Argynnis paphia Linnaeus

DISTRIBUTION: Europe, Algeria, across temperate Asia to Japan.

FOODPLANTS: Dog Violet (*Viola canina*) is the most favoured foodplant in the wild. Captive-bred larvae will take any of the violet family, including pansy.

GENERAL NOTES
The Silver-washed Fritillary is a common butterfly in Britain, being very prolific in the south and south-western counties, but it does not occur very far north of the Midlands. The butterflies feed from a variety of wild flowers, and spend long periods, flying or settled, high in the canopy of woodlands.

This is the largest British Fritillary, and has the truly beautiful flashing golden flight characteristic of our three larger species. From the underside coloration of the butterfly, it is easy to see why it was so named; the hindwings are green and streaked with silver, while the forewings have their tips suffused with green. The wings really do give the impression of having been painted with a watercolour wash.

Some broods of this single-brooded produce a very dark form, but only in the females (form *valesina*). This form, which is fairly common, has none of the brown coloration, but instead is a dull green.

Females do not lay eggs on the foodplant, but on trees nearby. Oak is often favoured because of its rough bark. Eggs are laid singly in cracks and crevices, usually close to the base of the tree.

The larvae hatch after about two weeks, and move into a suitable hiding place, where they spin a tiny patch of silk. They spend the winter hibernation on the silken pad, having eaten nothing except their eggshells. In the spring, the tiny caterpillars move out into the undergrowth in search of food. They finally mature towards the end of May, or early June. As with the other large Fritillaries, the caterpillars are quite large, and extremely beautiful. They have long spines along the back, and two horn-like projections just behind the head. Spines also project upwards and downwards from the spiracle, in the side of each segment, and fawn stripes run from head to tail. The caterpillars finally pupate, hanging from the cremaster.

Marsh Fritillary

Eurodryas aurinia Rottemburg

DISTRIBUTION: Europe through Russia to Korea.

FOODPLANTS: Devilsbit Scabious (*Succisa pratensis*) is the preferred foodplant, but captive-bred larvae will take other species, including Wild Honeysuckle (*Lonicera periclymenum*).

GENERAL NOTES

The Marsh Fritillary is distributed in the British Isles Britain in local pockets throughout England and Wales. A few isolated colonies exist in the west of Scotland. They are most common in the south-western counties of England, and in Ireland a much darker form can be found (form *hibernica*).

There is only one brood each year and, although damp or marshy ground is most suitable, this species will also frequent rough grassy situations, areas of scrubland, and open woodland where trees have recently been felled.

The female Marsh Fritillary is larger than the male, and the body is probably three times fatter. They are out towards the end of May, and can still be seen on the wing at the end of June.

The males are much more active than the females, the latter spending long periods settled, motionless. Eggs are either laid in large masses of several hundred, or in two smaller batches. On hatching, the larvae spin a dense silken web, and feed gregariously inside it. In spite of this, many fall prey to parasitic wasps, which reduce their numbers considerably.

When they are about half-grown, the caterpillars cluster in larger, closely knit masses at the base of the foodplants, and go into hibernation. In the spring, they continue to feed, and in some years they are so prolific that great masses of larvae have to wander in search of food.

The larva is short, dumpy and black in colour. It has short, bristly spines with small white spots peppering the sides. The back is also spotted, but to a lesser degree.

Pupation takes place in May, amongst the undergrowth, with the pupa hanging by the tail. The chrysalis is snub-nosed and greenish in colour; segments from the dorsal section to the end of the tail are striped black.

PAPILIONIDAE:
Swallowtails

European Swallowtail
Papilo machaon (ssp. *britannicus*) Linnaeus

DISTRIBUTION: Europe, north Africa, temperate Asia to Japan. Subspecies found throughout North America.

FOODPLANTS: Milk Parsley (*Peucedanum palustre*) is the principal foodplant. It will also lay on Angelica (*Angelica sylvestris*), Wild Carrot (*Daucus carota*) and Fennel (*Foeniculum vulgare*).

GENERAL NOTES

In England, the well-known Wicken Fen in Cambridgeshire was once a strongold of *machaon*, and efforts are being made to reintroduce it there. Biting north-easterly gales, combined with fen drainage, could have assisted in its decline, and it is now a protected species, being restricted to a few inaccessible locations in Norfolk. In the past it was more widespread in the fenlands of eastern England, and even in some southern counties. We can only hope that this scarce butterfly, the only British species of Papilionidae, will continue to hold its precarious place amongst our declining Lepidoptera.

This beauiful butterfly is out in May and June, and has a vigorous flight, often gliding down to feed on fenland flowers. The courtship display is spectacular, the pair spiralling upwards and downwards prior to mating. Once paired, the female sometimes flies with the male hanging limply beneath, to settle in a warm place.

The female lays her eggs singly under the edges of leaves, often returning to the same plant to lay again. She will patrol her territory to defend it against intruding butterflies. The mature larvae are typical of Papilionidae, and, if disturbed, produce a smooth, forked, orange organ (the osmaterium) from behind the head. This smells very strongly of burnt almonds, and acts as a deterrent to predators. The caterpillar is basically green, with tiger-like stripes and orange spots.

In July and August, the larvae pupate on sturdy reed stems. As with many overwintering pupae, they girdle themselves in an upright position to withstand winter gales. The pupae vary in colour from bright green to grey or brown, often blending with the colour of the pupation site. In warm seasons some pupae will emerge in August and produce a second brood, which, weather permitting, pupate in September.

2. Some Migratory Butterflies

Butterflies migrate from one place to another, even from one country to another, for a variety of reasons. Some have definite migratory tendencies and seem to enjoy flying great distances, either on a regular flight path or in no particular direction.

Others are extending their range in summertime because the higher temperatures permit them to do so.

In some instances individuals are carried by currents of air by accident and in certain years when breeding conditions are particularly favourable, great numbers may move *en masse* searching for fresh breeding grounds.

The following pages contain some of the better known species that for one reason or another often travel great distances.

PIERIDAE:
Whites and Sulphurs

Clouded Yellow
Colias croceus Geoffroy

DISTRIBUTION: Europe across Asia Minor to Iran, North Africa.

In Mediterranean countries, the Clouded Yellow is continuously brooded, and can be seen singly or in quite large numbers. In Britain, migrants usually arrive in May, and they continue to appear on occasion until September. Foodplants include Clover (*Trifolium*), Trefoil (*Lotus*), Melilot (*Melilotus*) and others. Plants most commonly used are clover and lucerne.

They are strong fliers, moving through one's field of vision with considerable speed, rather like male Brimstones in search of a spring female.

The male is bright yellow, with a heavy black border; there is also a slight black suffusion in the yellow, mostly on the hindwings. The female is slightly larger than the male, and her wing borders are dotted with yellow patches. These border markings are very variable, and collections used to be made containing vast series of specimens to illustrate these variations.

A percentage of each brood also produces pale, almost white females (form *helice*), and these have been confused with the Pale Clouded Yellow (*C. hyale*) (see below). However, the latter has a much narrower wing border.

Migrants gather in fields of clover and lucerne to lay their eggs, and, fully grown, the caterpillars are bright green with a yellow and red stripe down each side. Each segment carries a black spot just below the stripe, which creates a striking lateral pattern against the green body.

Pupation is succincti, held at the tail and girdled, often on the foodplant, and the chrysalis is greenish yellow with black markings on the underside of the abdomen.

Larvae still trying to feed towards the end of September die at the onset of autumn, but British-bred butterflies do appear in July and August. Being migrants, they can appear anywhere, but are more frequently found in the south.

Pale Clouded Yellow
Colias hyale Linnaeus

DISTRIBUTION: Europe to Altai Mountains, Abyssinia.

The male of this species is easily distinguished from the pale-coloured female, because it is a bright primrose yellow. All the other markings are virtually identical. They can be seen as early as May and June in Britain, but more likely later in the summer. They could appear in any southern coastal areas, but seem more common in Kent.

Females lay on lucerne, which is grown as a crop, and various clovers (*Trifolium*). The larvae progress through six instars to attain full growth; it is possible that a few are occasionally produced during the summer in Britain, although hibernation is impossible in our climate.

The mature larva is light green, and peppered with tiny black spots, each containing a single hair; this gives it a dusky tinge. The spiracles are white, encircled with a black line, and a bright yellow stripe containing orange blotches runs lengthwise down each side.

In Britain it is usually scarce. The best years for numbers officially recorded were 1900, when 2,200 were reported, and 1947, with 870 reports.

Berger's Clouded Yellow
Colias australis Verity

DISTRIBUTION: South and central Europe.

This species was separated from the Pale Clouded Yellow (*C. hyale*) (see above) in 1947 by L. A. Berger, hence the name. He recorded the much reduced black border on the hindwings of *C. australis*; the more rounded forewing, and the slightly larger discoidal spots on the hindwing. The spots are also a deeper orange on *C. australis*, and the small crescent markings near the outer margin are orange; they are much darker on *C. hyale*.

Berger's Clouded Yellow frequents chalk hillsides and downs, and this type of habitat sets it apart from *C. hyale* and *C. croceus* (see above), which would be found in fields of lucerne and clover.

Females lay on Horseshoe Vetch (*Hippocrepis comosa*), and the larvae have six or seven instars. They are easily distinguished from those of *C. hyale* by the two yellow lines with black spots running along the sides of the body instead of a single yellow and orange stripe. When ready to pupate, the caterpillar finds a sturdy stem, and pupates, girdled and fixed by the cremaster.

The chrysalis is bright green, with a row of tiny black spots across the wing cases. The underside of the abdomen is yellowish with black spotting.

Although summer breeding is possible, hibernation occurs in the larval form, and it is most unlikely that any have ever survived the British winter.

Bath White
Pontia daplidice Linnaeus

DISTRIBUTION: North Africa, south and central Europe to India and Japan.

The Bath White frequents open, rough situations, in Britain favouring the south-eastern counties of England. It is a very rare visitor, and a sighting in the wild is special indeed. Before 1945, only about 200 individuals had been noted, but in that year 650 were recorded.

The adults are similar to the Orange Tip (*Anthocharis cardamines*) (see page 32), but the black markings on *P. daplidice* are more extensive, especially on the female, and broken by white patches. The green underside markings are also much denser and smudged in appearance.

Eggs are laid on Mignonette (*Reseda lutea*) and Hedge Mustard (*Sisymbrium officinale*); the larvae have five instars.

The caterpillars are a bluish-grey, with raised black spots on which grow single black hairs. They have yellow lateral stripes, and the prolegs are also yellow.

The chrysalis is a similar colour to the larva, with a pointed head and tail; it is fixed to a stem by the tail, and girdled.

In good seasons, it is possible for this species to produce two broods, but they never manage to survive through the winter.

The Black-veined White

Aporia crataegi Linnaeus

DISTRIBUTION: Europe across temperate Asia to China and Japan.

This species has been extinct in Britain for about 50 years, although at one time it was regarded as a pest in orchards. The wing veining is very distinct on a greyish white base colour, and the female's wings are very sparsely scaled. The females lay their eggs on sloe, plum and other fruit trees, and the larvae hibernate while still very small, in a communal nest of silk. In the spring, they feed up through five instars to full growth; the caterpillar is grey with broad black and yellow lateral stripes, and covered in white and yellow hair. The chrysalis, which is held by the tail and girdled, is pale yellow with black spots and blotches, forming a pattern over the whole shell. The wing cases are well marked with a black border, and a row of black spots towards the outer margin.

LYCAENIDAE:
Blues, Coppers and Hairstreaks

Mazarine Blue
Cyaniris semiargus Rottemburg

DISTRIBUTION: Europe, Morocco, Asia to Mongolia.

These butterflies became extinct in England in the early part of this century, although it was once a localized species in the southern counties of England.

They prefer rough scrubland and open situations, where the foodplant occurs. The male of this migrant butterfly has a distinct purplish blue colour which is easily distinguished from any British residents; the female is a dullish brown, and the underside of both sexes is pale brown with some variable spotting.

The caterpillar is typical of the Blues, being green in colour, and it feeds on Red Clover, Kidney Vetch, and Melilot. It pupates succincti, girdled to a stem, and only one brood is produced each season.

Long-tailed Blue
Lampides boeticus Linnaeus

DISTRIBUTION: Temperate Europe, Japan, Africa, Australia.

Scorched grassy banks on the Costa del Sol are typical haunts of this species, so it is no wonder it is rarely seen in Britain. However, they do occasionally appear on the south coastal downs of England, and will produce British-bred butterflies in favourable seasons. They are continually brooded in the tropics, and the larvae feed on Everlasting Pea (*Lathyrus latifolius*), but they will also take other Leguminosae, and can be captive-bred on garden pea and lupins.

The male is bright blue with a narrow black border, and has a small eye-spot near the fine tail. The female is very dark, with a splash of iridescent blue on the fore- and hindwings. She also has three small eye-spots near the tail, and the underside of both sexes is pale with heavy, broken, buff striping.

The caterpillars are pale green with darker green lateral stripes, and they pupate loose at the base of the foodplant.

Short-tailed Blue

Everes argiades Pallas

DISTRIBUTION: Central Europe, Asia to Korea and Japan, India, Malaysia.

This species has been taken several times at Bloxworth in Dorset England, and is sometimes referred to as the Bloxworth Blue by British enthusiasts.

The male of this species is violet-blue, and the wing veins are quite clearly defined. He has a dark wing border, and very short, fine tails. The female is very dark brown, with two faint orange cresents near the tails, and the underside of both sexes is silvery white with black marginal spots running in two lines. Both sexes have heavier spotting at hindwing outer margins, broken by a pale orange bar.

The larvae, which are very pale green, feed on various parts of their foodplants, including the flowers; the foodplants include Birdsfoot Trefoil (*Lotus corniculatus*), and clovers. Pupation takes place loose at the base of the foodplant. This species has never been known to breed in Britain naturally.

DANAIDAE

Monarch or Milkweed
Danaus plexippus Linnaeus

DISTRIBUTION: Pacific Islands, Australasia, North America, Canary Isles.

This butterfly is more familiarly known as the Milkweed, since this is its foodplant. In America, it is known as the Monarch. It is bred every year by enthusiasts all over Britain; many are released or escape, but only a few species of the foodplant could survive our winters, and they would be governed by frost, which kills the foliage back to ground level in the winter.

The Monarch travels great distances, with migration routes stretching from Hudson's Bay in Canada, to Florida and southern California. In 1973, a huge hibernation site was discovered in Brazil. It has landed on ships almost 1,300km (800 miles) from any land, it often finds it way to England from America. In Australia its roaming habit has earned it the name of 'the Wanderer'.

The larval foodplant, *Asclepias*, is poisonous, and the caterpillars and butterflies retain the poison from the plants in their bodies, and it is interesting to note that some birds can taste how much poison is present in their bodies, eating only those individuals which have a tolerable level.

They roost in semi-hibernation in their millions, and flourish anywhere where the foodplant grows. They have moved into various Asian countries, and even in the sparsely vegetated Canary Isles one can see them floating over the palm trees in the colourful holiday complexes.

Some caterpillars have striking colours to warn possible predators that they are poisonous to eat. An example is *Danaus plexippus*, the famous Monarch butterfly.

NYMPHALIDAE:
Brush-footed

Camberwell Beauty
Nymphalis antiopa Linnaeus

DISTRIBUTION: Western Europe, temperate Asia, throughout
North America, Bhutan.

Its striking combination of rich cream, jet black and deep,
lustrous maroon, has made this butterfly one of our most
famous species. It is a migrant from Scandinavia, and is said
to arrive in Britain in timber consignments, moved while the
butterfly is hibernating amongst the logs. It also occurs in
Germany and America, where it is known as the Mourning
Cloak.

Foodplants are willow, sallow, birch and elm.

The species has never been known to breed in Britain
naturally, but captive breeding has been achieved many
times. Females lay on twigs and stems of the foodplant, in
batches from about 40 eggs to over 200. The larvae feed under
the protection of a mass of silk, webbing fresh supplies as
they move, and they remain so until pupation.

The caterpillars are very much like those of the Peacock
(*Inachis io*), but are larger and have a row of reddish blotches
along the back. At full growth, the caterpillar pupates, and
the chrysalis hangs by the cremaster from a silken pad.

Queen of Spain Fritillary
Argynnis (Issoria) lathonia Linnaeus

DISTRIBUTION: Western Europe, north Africa, Canary Isles,
central Asia, Himalayas to western China.

This butterfly does occasionally migrate to Britain, and has been known to breed there, but the winters are too long and severe for it to become a resident.

The larvae feed on violets, and two or even three broods are produced each season. The caterpillars have short spines, and are velvety black in colour, with tiny white spots peppered over the body.

The chrysalis, which hangs by the tail, is olive brown in colour with a narrow saddle of white.

3. BREEDING BUTTERFLIES

A question I am often asked is 'How difficult or easy is it to breed butterflies in captivity without a lot of space?' Very often individuals have been to a large walk-through butterfly house and, for the first time, have seen the complete life cycle of a butterfly from the egg through to the perfect adult insect. Interest is aroused and the beginner toys with the idea of breeding at home. Butterflies can be, to some extent, put into categories and slotted into various breeding methods. Native species can be bred very cheaply and for the beginner the hobby can be most rewarding and inexpensive.

GENERAL INFORMATION

Females lay their eggs on selected foodplants in very carefully chosen locations. Even if the foodplant is abundant, they will often take endless time and trouble to pick the exact spot to place their eggs.

As it is laid, the egg is covered with a natural gum which dries very quickly; this gives it protection, and also fixes it securely to the foodplant.

Eggs are as variable as snowflakes in their shape, texture and colour. Their elaborate structure is best seen under a microscope, when they appear netted or grooved, often resembling shell, porcelain or even silk.

Some females lay their eggs singly, others in great masses of over 200 and, with few exceptions, they are placed in a position which offers maximum protection against the elements and dangers of nature.

As the embryo grows it can often be seen curled up inside the transparent shell, with the head prominently visible. Eggs are very delicate and should never be handled unless it is absolutely necessary. If purchased or collected, it is important to ensure that they are not allowed to dry out. This can be achieved by keeping them in a small plastic box with a well-fitting lid. Each day prior to hatching, lift the lid and release a long, slow breath of air on to the eggs. The inside of the box will now be steamed up and this will supply the eggs with the humidity they need.

On hatching the larvae invariably eat their eggshells. To most larvae this is essential, and if disturbed and prevented from doing so they will die.

Caterpillars come in a bewildering variety of shapes and colours, many species changing colour between skin changes. On average, they change skins five times, and the period between each is called an instar. Never handle small caterpillars – a small soft-bristled brush should be used to transfer them gently to the foodplant.

When changing foodplants, try to arrange it so that the caterpillars can move themselves on to fresh food. If this is not possible, handle them with a brush, but never move a caterpillar that is about to shed its skin. At this time it has anchored itself to the foodplant with a carpet of silk, spun from glands near the jaw. If removed from the silk, the skin change will be difficult, and sometimes proves impossible, resulting in death.

Caterpillars have no bones; their bodies are manipulated by about 2,000 tiny muscles. They have a head followed by three segments which form the thorax, and a further 10 segments which form the abdomen. The thoracic segments each carry a pair of single-clawed legs and five of the abdominal segments carry a pair of fleshy false legs, known as prolegs. The rear segment carries the powerful claspers, and if you must remove a caterpillar from a plant make sure the claspers are not holding; the body can break in two before their grip is released.

A golden rule when rearing caterpillars is to keep the container clean, and change cut food *every* day. If you keep strictly to this rule you will have success.

The final larval skin change reveals the chrysalis or pupa. During this stage the dramatic final transformation from caterpillar to butterfly takes place: the metamorphosis.

Caterpillars often spend hours searching for a safe place to pupate, and at this stage many are taken by predators. Larvae pupate in different ways. Some spin a pad of silk on the foodplant or away in the undergrowth. Before shedding their skin they hang from the silken pad, holding on with the claspers. On a natural weak point, just behind the head, the larval skin breaks and slowly the chrysalis (or pupa) appears. The tail of the chrysalis is lined with tiny hooks (cremaster), and as it twists free of the shed skin, the hooks catch and anchor to the pad. The still soft chrysalis twists and turns until the discarded skin falls away.

This method of pupation is called suspensi (suspended). The Admirals, Fritillaries and Vanessids (Nymphalidae) all pupate suspensi.

Most of the butterflies which hibernate as pupae secure themselves more firmly, by adding further support in the form of a silken girdle. This fixes the chrysalis in a horizontal or upright position and is called succincti (girdled). About half the Skippers (Hesperiidae), all the Whites and Sulphurs (Pieridae) and the Swallowtails (Papilionidae) pupate succincti.

Other caterpillars spin flimsy cocoons or pupate on the ground without any restrictive support; this method is called involuti (loose). The remaining Skippers and all the Blues, Coppers and Hairstreaks (Lycaenidae) pupate involuti.

Pupae are delicate and must be handled with great care. It is best to leave them in the pupation position to emerge. However, if movement is unavoidable, cut away the sections of plant complete with chrysalis and pin it up in a cage to emerge. Pupae that have to be removed from a plant should be moved complete with silken pad still attached to the cremaster. They can then be glued or pinned up to emerge. As a last resort, place them loose in an emerging cage.

The construction of an emerging cage is illustrated in Fig. 1. The distance from the base to the top of an emerging cage should be as short as possible. Butterflies climb to the 'ceiling' of their cage on emerging, where they hang upside down to pump up their wings; therefore, the shorter the distance they must travel to do this the better. The corrugated cardboard on which the pupae lie should be kept damp at all times.

'Colouring up' is an expression used by butterfly breeders to describe the pupal case when emergence is imminent. The case often turns completely transparent, allowing the wing markings, the result of pigment appearing in the wing scales, to show through. A good example of this is the Monarch (*Danaus plexippus*). This has a bright emerald green pupa which turns transparent revealing the brilliant colours of the butterfly inside.

When the butterfly is ready to emerge the pupal skin splits

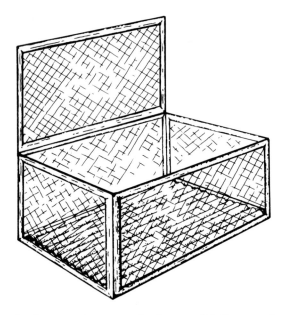

Fig. 1.   In the emerging cage, the floor–to–lid distance should be as short as possible; the freshly emerged butterflies will hang on to the lid in order to pump up their wings. Corrugated cardboard in the base should be kept dampened. An adequate size is 20 × 30cm and 15cm (8 × 12 × 6in) high.

just behind the head. After freeing its legs and antennae, the perfect insect slips ever so gently from the pupal case, often suspending itself from the empty husk to pump up its wings.

At first the wings are crumpled, soft and damp, comprising two limp membranes fused together and supported by flexible veins. By hanging upside down, gravity assists to force blood through the veins, slowly expanding and flattening the wings. When fully expanded the wings are held slightly apart to dry. When they are hardened the blood is withdrawn from the wings, and the butterfly is ready for its maiden flight.

During the pumping up process excretory liquid, that has accumulated in the digestive tract during pupation, is released from the anus. This liquid is usually bright red or yellow. If a sprayer is used to give extra humidity in a flight cage, care should be taken never to spray pupae about to emerge. The sudden shock of water invariably causes the premature release of the excretory liquid into the pupal case, resulting in the butterfly being unable to emerge. At any other time, however, light spraying is beneficial.

HOUSING FOR CAPTIVE BREEDING

The same methods of culture can be used with success for a wide variety of different species. The equipment needed can be simple and inexpensive, or as sophisticated and costly as the breeder wants to make it.

For example, some of our most colourful species, such as the Red Admiral, Peacock, Small Tortoiseshell and Comma, will mate and produce eggs in a garden tub containing the larval foodplant, with black nylon mesh stretched and secured across the top. They will also breed in a large flower pot which contains the foodplant, encapsulated with black nylon mesh supported by hoops of wire.

The same species can also be bred in an expensive greenhouse, planted out with nectar-producing flowers, and foodplants for egg-laying.

In the following pages, several techniques of breeding are explained, and these can be applied to many species.

Tub Breeding

If butterflies are taken from the wild, the females will almost certainly have been fertilized already; therefore, it is not necessary to capture males. To ensure that sufficient eggs are produced, introduce several females into the tub.

The tub need not be large – an ideal size would be 40cm (16in) in diameter, and 35cm (14in) deep, as illustrated (Fig. 2). This would be quite suitable for the species listed on page 114.

The larval foodplant can be planted directly in the tub, provided it has the correct growing medium to become well-established and healthy in readiness for the butterflies.

Feeding your butterflies correctly is most important, and

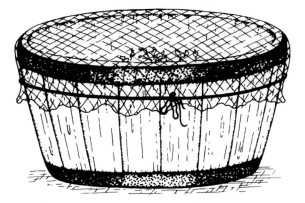

Fig. 2. The breeding tub will produce eggs from many butterfly species and provides a simple and rewarding method.

this is achieved by mixing a solution of water, honey or fruit sugar (fructose), the latter two ingredients not exceeding 5 per cent. Cotton wool pads should then be soaked in this artificial nectar and placed on top of the nylon mesh. Fresh pads must be put out every day, and the nylon mesh must be kept taut across the tub.

Many of the species listed will complete their life cycle using the tub method of breeding, but if too many are produced, they will have to be transferred to a fresh foodplant when their supply is exhausted.

This breeding method is ideal for species which overwinter as eggs or larvae, but take care how and where the tub is placed. Many species choose sheltered, sloping situations in which to hibernate; others prefer the most harsh and exposed conditions. If a sheltered situation is required, tilt the tub into a position which will catch the maximum amount of sunlight, and place it out of the wind. However, overwintering eggs may need cold winds and open conditions to prevent early hatching. If this is the case, remove the foodplant and repot it, then place it in an open, airy mesh cage, and put the cage in an open situation.

The tub method is well suited for breeding Hairstreaks, because of its circular construction. These butterflies tend to

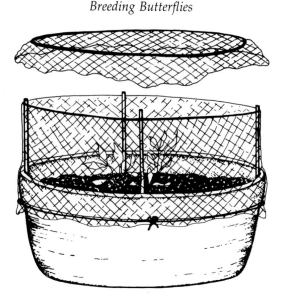

Fig. 3. The extended tub provides more space for the larger foodplants and can even contain small saplings.

become trapped in corners, and often starve; obviously, with this method, there are no corners to trap them. Another problem with Hairstreaks is the foodplant: young trees have to be used for egg-laying and it is difficult to put an oak tree in a 40cm (16in) tub. To make this easier, an extension can be fitted to the tub (see Fig. 3). The extra room for young trees, created by the extension, makes it ideal for Hairstreaks. With the exception of the Green Hairstreak, they all hibernate in egg form on the terminal leaves and stems of the foodplant. The extension elevates the eggs out of the shelter of the tub, making overwintering conditions perfect.

SPECIES SUITABLE FOR THE TUB METHOD

All the Hairstreaks	Duke of Burgundy Fritillary
All the Skippers	Small Pearl-bordered Fritillary
Small Copper	Pearl-bordered Fritillary
Small Blue	Marsh Fritillary
Common Blue	Glanville Fritillary
Chalkhill Blue	Heath Fritillary
Adonis Blue	

If they should consume all the foodplant in the tub, these species do not require specialist treatment; they just have to be moved on to fresh food, so always ensure that fresh potted food is available.

In addition to those listed above, the following species can be bred using the tub, but the larvae need special feeding arrangements (see pages 126–30):

Red Admiral   Large Tortoiseshell
Painted Lady   Peacock
Small Tortoiseshell   Comma

Flower Pots or Small Cages

Both these methods are also suitable for some of the species listed under the tub method.

The flower pot and small cage really do the same job, and it is a matter of personal choice which one to use.

Foodplants are planted in the flower pot, and black nylon mesh supported by wire keeps the butterflies captive while they produce eggs (see Fig. 4).

With the small cage, a potted foodplant should be placed inside, ensuring that some of the leaves are against the black mesh (see Fig. 5).

Butterflies are collected and released into the appropriate container, and fed by way of the cotton wool pads soaked in honey or fruit sugar and water. If the species being bred overwinters as larvae, these can be left in either of the containers, provided they are placed in a suitable position. Most of the species listed will complete their life cycle with these methods, especially the grass feeders, but it is best to have established plants ready to use if required.

SPECIES SUITABLE FOR TUB, FLOWER POT AND SMALL CAGE METHODS
Small Copper   Common Blue
Small Blue

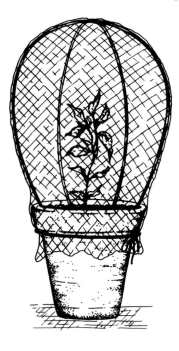

Fig. 4. The flower pot must be the easiest and least expensive container for breeding many butterfly species.

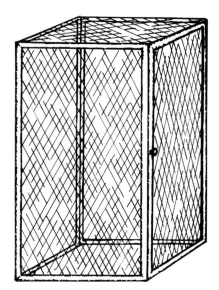

Fig. 5. A small cage will serve the same purpose as the flower pot and may be preferred. An ideal size would be 25 × 25cm and 35cm (10 × 10 × 14in) high.

SPECIES BETTER SUITED TO THE FLOWER POT AND SMALL CAGE ONLY

Silver-studded Blue   Gatekeeper
Brown Argus   Meadow Brown
Speckled Wood   Small Heath
Wall Brown   Large Heath
Scotch Argus   Ringlet

Large Breeding Cages

Some species are better suited to a larger cage and, with the extra space, cut flowers can be placed inside as well as the larval foodplant. A cage is illustrated as a guide (Fig. 6), but do experiment and make up a cage as large as you have room for.

Cut flowers should be changed every day, but some species, especially buddleia, will last longer if the stems are set in boiling water prior to being introduced. Pads of cotton wool soaked in the solution of honey, or fruit sugar and water can be placed on top and inside the cage, but bright colours in the form of artificial flowers may have to be incorporated with the pads to attract the butterflies.

Place the foodplants and some of the flowers against the mesh sides of the cage. This will encourage the captives to feed and lay eggs. Once eggs have been produced, they should be removed and placed in small plastic boxes to hatch. Larvae can then be reared in separate cages in a cooler, more suitable situation.

SPECIES BETTER SUITED TO THE LARGER BREEDING CAGE

Swallowtail   Orange Tip
Wood White   White Admiral
Clouded Yellow   High Brown Fritillary
Brimstone   Dark Green Fritillary
Large White   Silver-washed Fritillary
Small White   Monarch
Green-veined White

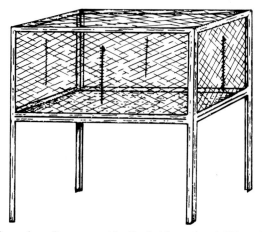

Fig. 6.   A large breeding cage, ideally (without legs) 150 × 50cm and 60cm (5ft × 1ft 8in × 2ft) high. Zippered openings, as indicated, are required for access.

Many of the species listed on page 117 overwinter as newly-hatched or partly-grown larvae. Conditions which they would encounter in the wild have to be reproduced as well as possible, to assist their hibernation.

For example, Purple Emperor larvae have to be reared on a sleeved, broad-leaved sallow (*Salix caprea*). At the third instar, the larvae go into hibernation, even changing from green to brown, creating perfect camouflage. Check that the sallow is healthy and free from mould, remove the sleeve and place the foodplant in a sheltered situation. In the spring, as soon as the buds begin to open, replace the sleeve and bring the plant into a sheltered site out of the wind in broken sunlight.

Sleeving is the use of nylon mesh sleeve which is pulled over a leafy branch upon which your caterpillars are feeding. It is tied at both ends to prevent escape. When the leaves of the branch are eaten, the caterpillars are moved to another branch and re-sleeved.

The Large Flight Cage

For the really keen enthusiast, the large flight cage can be a

Fig. 7. The large flight cage has a mesh ceiling beneath a transparent, corrugated plastic roof; a gap of 15cm (6in) is needed between the two. As a guide to size, the example illustrated is 1.8 × 1.5m (6 × 5ft) and some 1.8m (6ft) high to the plastic roof. Air vents should be provided in the wooden base. The floor may be the natural ground, or boarded if this is preferred.

real joy. Study the illustration (Fig. 7); the basic idea of size, with the double venting roof, is a tried and trusted method that works well.

The wooden fascia around the base will draw plants up quickly where they are needed, and also keep the butterflies off the floor. In a cage of this size, five or six species can be bred at one time, and the benefit for both keeper and butterflies is that they can fly and feed naturally.

It is advisable to have all, or most, of the plants in pots and tubs, as they can then be moved in and out of your flight cage. This is very useful if any diseases or aphid infestations occur. Try to create a natural open area in the centre of the cage, by placing the larger plants around the edges and in the rear corners; this will encourage the butterflies to behave more naturally.

The large flight cage is really good to experiment with: it brings your hobby to life, and taxes the imagination. I have seen large flight cages produce great masses of surplus larvae that can be sold to other enthusiasts, to help pay for even larger cages, perhaps even a greenhouse. With a greenhouse, the amateur can then diversify to exotic butterflies, but that is a very different story!

The Greenhouse Method

Some exotic species need the space and warmth of a heated greenhouse for continued success. This means that the breeder is creating a mini-environment in a climate that would normally be alien to the captives inside.

This, in itself, can cause enormous problems if the greenhouse is in constant use, usually brought about by unwanted pests such as thrips, mealy-bugs, white fly and scale insects.

Because the greenhouse is so perfect an insect breeding environment, pests take full advantage of the situation and can, once admitted, reach plague proportions. The worst offenders are mealy-bug, scale insects and white fly; all these leave sticky secretions on food plants, especially *Passiflora* and *Citrus*. The dirty leaves attract dust and bacteria; your precious caterpillars eat the leaves, and soon deaths start to occur as bacteria find their way into the gut of your caterpillars. As if this is not bad enough, some infected caterpillars survive to become butterflies, and infections are passed on to the next generation, coated on to the eggshells which the newly hatched caterpillars invariably eat. In this way whole breeding stocks can be wiped out. So what can we do?

Firstly, prevention is better than cure. I have found it useful if a cap-full of a mild antiseptic liquid (such as T.C.P.) is diluted in a hand sprayer full of water and sprayed liberally on foodplants, paying particular attention to areas of the plant covered in eggs and caterpillars. If this is carried out once every week it is unlikely that bacteria will attain levels that will cause problems.

In a heated greenhouse foodplants can be infected by white fly as soon as they are put in. Here are some *Danaus plexippus* caterpillars feeding on *Asclepias curassavica*.

EGG STERILIZATION

The scientific way to prevent bacteria, however, is to sterilize the eggs. The most popular chemical for the job is formaldehyde, and its use in egg sterilization was perfected by Mr Claude Rivers, formerly of Oxford University. Equipment needed is a bottle of formaldehyde, a box of soft tissues or soft toilet tissue and a fine plastic tea strainer. The method used is as follows.

Formaldehyde, when purchased from a chemist, is usually at a strength of 40 per cent. This has to be further reduced to 10 per cent by dilution in water – 3 measures of water to one of formaldehyde. The liquid is then placed in a shallow container.

Butterfly eggs are collected and placed in the plastic tea strainer which in turn is lowered into the solution and waggled about to attain the eggs' total submersion; they are left submerged for 40 minutes. After this period of time, remove the eggs and gently wash them in clean tepid water using the tea strainer again as a holding receptacle. When washed, carefully dry the eggs with paper tissue and place them in a plastic box to hatch, as described on page 107.

The formaldehyde will have killed any bacteria on the eggshell surface leaving it sterile and clean. It also hardens the eggshells.

Another solution that has been used in the same way is baby bottle sterilization liquid (such as Milton). With these liquids the dilution is more difficult being 0.2 per cent, and they tend to soften the eggshells if they are submerged for longer than eight minutes.

Formaldehyde is also used for pickling dead creatures – nice to see it being used for something living instead.

The cause of all these problems, dirty food plants, must be eliminated if success is to be attained. It goes without saying, that if the newly hatched caterpillars from sterilized eggs are placed on to dirty foodplants problems will recur.

The Double Greenhouse Method for Heliconid Species

This is an expensive method to set up but works very well. The idea is to have one greenhouse for summer breeding and the other for winter breeding.

The summer house can be set up directly over garden soil; the best results are obtained with houses 2.4 × 3m (8 × 10ft) or larger. The entire inside of the greenhouse should be lined with plastic bubble packing material, which is a good insulation against the cold. Two layers of this insulation should be used, each strip should be overlapped by 5cm (2in) and all the edges should be sealed with plastic tape.

Passion flower vines (for breeding Heliconiidae) can be planted along one side of the house and various nectar flowers along the other. The vines should be allowed to make considerable growth before the introduction of butterflies. With five vines in a 2.4 × 3m (8 × 10ft) greenhouse a colony of *Heliconius melpomone* will grow from one pair to about 1,000 plus individuals from June to October. As the colony grows, food must be provided for the butterflies (see page 117).

At the end of October the whole colony should be removed to the winter greenhouse. It should be set up as the first one, but have at least three or four layers of insulation.

By the end of October the foodplant in your second greenhouse will be in prime condition. During the summer months the vines should be trained up to the apex of the greenhouse to hang in loops of wire. Two fan heaters of at least 2 kW can now be put into operation working on a thermostat set at 27°C (80°F) blowing across the floor from either end of the house.

The winter greenhouse works more efficiently if lighting is added. Three 1.5m (5ft) white strip lights and one UVA blue light should be fitted on a time switch. The timer should be set to come on at 06.00 and switch off at 15.00 hours; this will allow for a natural twilight, during which time the flock will hang up for the night.

Butterflies bred during the winter are smaller than those bred in summertime, but if these directions are followed, this double greenhouse method will work indefinitely. It is an ideal method for the professional in conjunction with a butterfly exhibition and will ensure that these beautiful butterflies are a constant joy to the visitor.

The golden rule is light, heat and good quality foodplant at all times, all the year round, without exception.

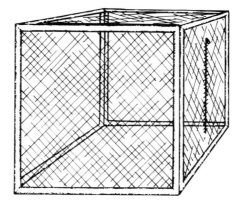

Fig. 8. An indoor Heliconid breeding cage, which should be no smaller than 1.8 × 1.5m (6 × 5ft), and 1.8m (6ft) high. The illustrated example is a 2-metre (6ft 6in) cube with zippered access.

Breeding in the Home

If you have a conservatory or even a spare room it is quite simple to set up a breeding area.

Construct a wooden frame no smaller than 2 × 1.2m and 2m high (6 × 4 × 6ft) but as large as your room will allow. Cover the frame with a good quality black nylon mesh with a large zip for the entrance (see Fig. 8).

Do not use walls or windows as part of your breeding cage. These can become cold to touch and when a butterfly settles the cold will weaken it. Preferably place your cage well away from walls or windows.

Lighting can be provided with strip lights – two or three 1.5m (5ft) strip lights and one UVA blue light mounted above your cage — these must be switched off about an hour before dark to allow for a natural twilight.

Heating is usually provided by a thermostatically controlled electric fan heater inside the cage, as described for the double greenhouse method.

Feeding the butterflies is achieved using a combination of methods. Blue, yellow or red shallow plastic containers are filled with cotton wool soaked in a mixture of honey or fruit sugar and water, 5 per cent honey (or fruit sugar) and 95 per cent water. The mixture and cotton wool should be changed daily. The containers need to be about 1.2m (4ft) from the ground, hanging from wires or on pedestals.

Cut flowers in water or flowers growing in pots are needed to provide pollen. Cut flowers should be changed after two days. Pollen can be purchased from health shops both in granule and tablet form; tablets can be crushed and sprinkled on the honey-soaked cotton wool.

Your colony size will be dependent on how many potted *Passiflora* vines you can provide, allowing for a rotation of your plant stock. As soon as there are sufficient eggs on one plant, it should be taken out of the cage and replaced with a fresh one. The healthier and fresher your food plants the stronger and larger will be your butterflies.

BREEDING METHODS FOR SOME TEMPERATE SPECIES

Small Tortoiseshell and Peacock

These larvae feed in large webbed clusters until the final instar, preferring new growth to older, tougher leaves. Use of the tub method will bring the larvae to their second or third instar. They can now be introduced to the rearing container (Fig. 9). A brood of 150 larvae can be reared using this cage.

Cut a bunch of fresh nettle, approximately 75cm (30in) long, just a little longer than the depth of the cage. Secure the cut end of the bunch with string or a strong elastic band, and hang it upside down in the cage from the central strut.

The nettle should be changed daily and provided in increasing quantity as the larvae grow. Changing the foodplant is a surprisingly easy operation: shake the old nettle, and the larvae will fall to the cage floor. Place the old nettle in another cage, so that any larvae awaiting skin changes can be removed the next day. Put in the fresh nettle and the larvae will quickly move up into the leaves. When they have done so, gently remove the nettle again, complete with larvae, and empty the droppings from the cage. Finally, place the fresh food with the larvae back into the cage, and replace the top.

When the larvae begin to pupate, most will do so on the mesh top. However, some will inevitably pupate on the nettle. Take care not to discard pupae with the old foodplant.

Do experiment with other methods of rearing – it all makes the hobby more interesting. However, if you do, never place nettle into water in the hope that it will last longer; too much water is taken up by the plant and consequently by the larvae, so that most of them will die just prior to pupation.

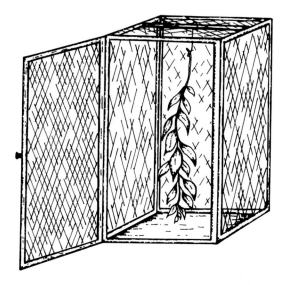

Fig. 9. The Small Tortoiseshell and Peacock rearing cage. The base is wooden, with all-mesh sides and top, and there is a hook for foodplants hanging from a central strut. An ideal size would be 30 × 30cm and 74cm (12 × 12 × 29in) high.

BREEDING LARGE NUMBERS

The enthusiast may wish to breed large numbers of Peacock or Small Tortoiseshell butterflies for release, or other reasons. The larger breeding cage (Fig. 10). is designed for this purpose.

Instead of using one bunch of foodplant, three can be used in rotation. Start in the same way as with the smaller cage, by placing one bunch of nettle, but this time cut just a little shorter than the cage depth. Hang the first nettle to one side of the cage.

On day two, place the second bunch in the middle of the cage, and leave the first one in place. Each day thereafter, take out the oldest bunch, which will now be withered; and devoid of larvae. Move the remaining two bunches along the central strut, so that the previous day's food is now in the centre, then place the fresh foodplant in the vacant space.

127

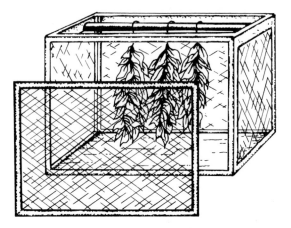

Fig. 10.   A larger scale cage for Small Tortoiseshells and Peacocks. There is space for three sets of foodplants, which can be rotated each day; one in, one out. An ideal size would be 75 × 37cm and about 30cm (30 × 15× 12in) deep.

Using this method, the larvae will not have to be disturbed when changing skin, and, because the cage is large and the nettle is not touching the floor, droppings need only be cleaned out after each brood. Ensure that the bunches are just touching, to allow the larvae to move freely on to fresh food. This larger cage will produce up to 500 pupae each time.

Large Tortoiseshell

This butterfly will produce eggs using the tub method, fitted with the extension (Fig. 3), and a small sallow planted inside. Make sure that there is plenty of leaf contact on the mesh sides.

Once eggs are produced, the larvae do best on growing food, sleeving being the best method of rearing.

If you can still find elm, they can be reared successfully on the cut foodplant, but sallow and willow need changing every few hours, because they do not keep fresh in water.

Red Admiral, Painted Lady and Comma

The larvae of these three species spend their lives in solitary hiding. The Red Admiral conceals itself by drawing the edges of a leaf together with silk to form a tent. Painted Lady larvae also draw a leaf together with silk and feed from the underside. Comma larvae just keep to the underside, feeding away from the edge, leaving the leaf perforated.

The Comma and the Painted Lady will take several different foodplants, but I have always used stinging nettles for all three species.

The tub method will induce the butterflies to produce eggs, and the larvae will progress through at least two instars. By this time the foodplant will be mostly eaten, and it will be time to move them into the special rearing container (Fig. 11).

Between 30 and 40 larvae can be reared at a time using this method, and the containers only have to be cleaned out once, after each brood.

Place a large paper kitchen towel in the bottom of the box, and a small sprig of nettle (just three or four leaves) in the centre. Using a small soft-bristled brush, tickle the caterpillars from the old leaves on to the fresh. The trick is to judge the

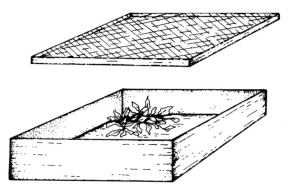

Fig. 11. The shallow tray method for the Red Admiral, Painted Lady and Comma should be 60 × 45cm and only 15cm (24 × 17× 6in) high.

129

eating requirements, which will of course increase daily, adding just slightly more than enough to satisfy their needs. After about 15 days, depending on temperature, pupae will suddenly appear, hanging from the mesh top of the container.

It really is that simple. When all the larvae have pupated, clean out the container thoroughly, and place a clean paper towel in the bottom to absorb any fluid released by your newly emerged butterflies.

Replace the top, complete with pupae, which will be hanging like sentinels from the mesh. The butterflies will emerge about 10 days later.

BREEDING METHODS FOR EXOTIC SPECIES

Papilionidae

There are about 700 species of Papilionids worldwide, containing the largest and most beautiful butterflies. Amongst these are the Birdwings (*Ornithoptera*) of the Australian region with dazzling colours in green and gold. The Pale Apollos (*Parnassius*) of the northern hemisphere can fly at very high altitudes, and the many brilliantly coloured species of the African and Indonesian regions and the South Americas decorate rain forests and suburban gardens alike.

The larvae feed on *Citrus* and *Aristolochia* and a wide range of foodplants; they are very similar in shape, though they vary a great deal in size and colour. They have a retractable organ called an osmaterium behind the head which is produced when the larva is disturbed, releasing a pungent odour.

The Swallowtails all pupate in the same way, fixed to a silken pad by the cremaster with a silken girdle around the middle (succincti).

On average a healthy Papilionid butterfly will live for about three weeks. The male is capable of mating several times; many of the females produce over 200 eggs. Usually the larger the butterfly the fewer eggs it will lay. The caterpillars are voracious feeders, a good quantity of healthy foodplants is needed to breed in any numbers.

Many species of Papilionidae are now available from entomological dealers. Some are easy to breed, others are difficult and not recommended unless required just for emerging and flying and not to breed. Dealers are usually aware of these and will recommend more suitable species.

A fully grown caterpillar of *Papilio aegeus aegeus* from Australia (above left).

A caterpillar of *Papilio aegeus aegeus* ready to pupate (above right)

This handsome chrysalis of *Papilio aegeus aegeus* is now ready for the final stage, the emergence.

The two main foodplants are *Citrus* and *Aristolochia*. *Citrus* feeders will take a variety of substitute foodplants such as *Choisya ternata*, *Skimmia* and *Ruta graveolens* if *Citrus* is not available; however, problems often occur after two or three broods when the larvae are fed on substitute foodplants. It may be that the strain weakens and the caterpillars are then susceptible to viral and/or bacterial infection; whether this is the case or not, the failure to produce healthy pupae is often put down to one of these reasons. The fact still remains that if caterpillars start dying when on a substitute foodplant and they are transferred on to *Citrus*, very often the change transforms the health and growth of the larvae and failure is turned to success. It could well be that there are no long-term substitute foodplants, only short-term ones.

To confirm my theories on this matter I have, on several occasions, bred a species through two generations but on the third, when troubles have usually occurred for me in the past, I have put half the larvae back on to *Citrus* and kept the rest on the substitute food. On each occasion the latter have died and the former produced healthy pupae.

Having said all this doom and gloom, do use substitute foodplants if *Citrus* is not available. Much enjoyment can be found breeding these beautiful butterflies. The easiest species for the beginner must be *Papilio polytes* from India and they will fly and breed in quite a small area.

I feel it only fair to say that one really needs a greenhouse to breed exotic Papilionids; temperature depends on the country of origin but 24° to 27°C (75° to 80°F) is a good guide to most of the species available.

They all thrive better when supplied with flowers for nectar, and the correct potted foodplant should be provided for egg laying. Honey or fruit sugar and water can be used to make sure the captives have sufficient food (5 per cent honey or fruit sugar, 95 per cent water) which can be introduced soaked into cotton wool pads placed in brightly coloured plastic containers. The greenhouse should be well insulated, free from draughts and, if necessary, heated to the required temperature with an electric fan heater.

Eggs are laid singly, mostly under the rim of the leaf; they are round in appearance and stuck firmly with a natural gum. Hatching is dependent on temperature, but in favourable conditions they should hatch within seven days. With many species the head of the larvae can be clearly seen as a black dot a day or so prior to hatching.

Papilionid larvae are quite robust and are easy to transfer from one plant to another with the aid of a small paintbrush. If substitute foodplants are to be used greater success will be achieved if the larvae are allowed to eat *Citrus* through the first instar. As far as I know there are no substitute foodplants for *Aristolochia* feeders.

If *Citrus* is difficult to obtain, it is well worth mentioning that lemon and orange pips will readily germinate in small flower pots in a good compost soil and kept in a warm kitchen. Butterflies will lay on these seedlings and go through the first instar easily. After the plants have been stripped of leaves, they will recover and grow with most green-fingered individuals.

If possible pupa are best left in their pupating position to emerge. If this is not possible they should be carefully removed and placed in an emerging cage on damp corrugated cardboard to emerge (see Fig. 1).

Though I have bred many hundreds of Papilionid over the years, and have even cross-bred species from different continents (though that was accidental), they are not my personal favourites. Given the choice and breeding for my own enjoyment, my greenhouses would all contain a different family of butterflies – the Heliconiidae from South America.

Heliconiidae

Heliconid butterflies are, without a doubt, *the* most rewarding species to breed. They are widely bred in butterfly farms and the amateur will often try to emulate the experts and set up colonies at home only to lose them in the winter. Why are Heliconids the species to breed? They live a very long time: I have had individuals flying for up to eight or nine months. The popular species, – *Heliconius melpomone* and *Heliconius erato* – are very easy on foodplants whereas other species – *Agraulis vanillae* or *Dryas julia* need more foodplant, making colony continuity much more difficult.

Before I explain further breeding methods for Heliconids it may help, and be of interest, to learn a little of the Heliconid's existence in the wild.

There are approximately 70 neotropical species found throughout South America. They are distaseful species, able to emit a pungent odour from a gland in the abdomen, and appear to advertise this fact by being brightly coloured and also by having an unusually lazy flight; their wings only move through a few degrees from the horizontal. Having said this, their flight is well-controlled; they can hover for long periods and even fly backwards.

When roosting at night individuals will select the most slender perches from which they hang upside down to sleep. Some species – *Heliconius charitonius* and *Heliconius erato*, for example – will congregate in flocks and hang in bunches.

With the first rays of sunshine in a new day, the first butterflies on the wing fly around touching others as if to wake them up. Soon there is a flurry of movement and colour before dispersing, each on its separate way. What is most strange is that the butterflies return to the same roost each night, often to the same perch throughout their lives.

They live much longer than other butterflies because of their unique ability to digest pollen which is a rich source of protein. Other butterfly families take food only in the form of liquids: for example, nectar, water from damp earth, tree sap from bruised trees. Most of these food sources supply energy but not protein in sufficient quantities to sustain long life. Heliconids on the other hand feed on nectar and pollen, the latter in large quantities; they also digest it in a unique way.

There is much competition between individuals early in the day to find pollen. It is collected by tiny hairs attached to the tongue (proboscis) which can soon be visible to the human eye as a sticky yellow mass. The butterfly eventually settles in a shady spot and secretes a powerful digestive enzyme from the tongue. Close examination at this stage reveals that the tongue is coiling and uncoiling slowly. This action (which I can only describe as being like a wrist-watch hair spring in slow motion) mixes the pollen into the secreted enzyme which is then ingested. This method of pollen feeding is unique to Heliconid butterflies and the added protein in their diet enables them to live longer than any other species. Many generations can be flying together.

Most butterflies mate and lay their eggs over a short period of time, some within as little as two or three weeks; not so the Heliconids. They lay their eggs over a much longer period, perhaps as long as six months. Work this out at an average of six to nine eggs per day and we have well over 1,000 eggs. Why, we may now ask, is not South America knee-deep in Heliconid butterflies? The answer lies in the fascinating relationship evolved between the larvae, black ants and their foodplant, passion flower vines (*Passiflora*).

Before laying, females of *Heliconius melpomone* and *Heliconius erato* first reconnoitre the vines to see how many eggs are already deposited. Once a certain density is reached they will not lay, as if knowing that the vine can only support so many caterpillars. This is beneficial to the foodplant and also ensures that the larvae always have sufficient food. Some of the *Passiflora* vines have evolved to produce tiny yellow patches on the leaves, also tiny nodules on the leaf stems, both of which resemble eggs. Entomologists think that these deter butterflies from laying. However, it is the tiny nodules on the leaf stems that hold the real key to the natural culling of these prolific species.

The nodules are, in fact, supplementary nectaries and produce tiny globules of sweet sticky honeydew. The honeydew attracts a ferocious species of omnivorous black ant. While the ants forage amongst the vines in enormous numbers they not only feed on the honeydew but also on the eggs and small caterpillars of the Heliconid butterflies. To see the trails of ants leaving the vines carrying their spoils makes one wonder how any butterflies survive at all.

The vines produce long snake-like tendrils to support their flimsy stems. Many of these tendrils can be over 30cm (12in) long and just a small percentage of the females lay their eggs on the tips of such tendrils. Ants rarely venture along these slender growths, feeling insecure. Consequently, eggs so deposited hatch unmolested and the tiny caterpillars begin to feed from the tip of the tendril.

The conversion from plantfood to caterpillar growth is rapid with this family and the caterpillar progresses through its five instars very quickly, pupating, very often still on its tendril, after as little as two to three weeks. Only very few of the eggs laid survive in this way, running the gauntlet of the ants to complete their life cycle. Nature will always find a way to bring about a balance.

Looking at the situation from the ants' point of view, the caterpillars and eggs must be a very important source of easy food supply and without these predators the caterpillars could well decimate their own food source.

To breed these beautiful butterflies continuously is not easy, but it is a most rewarding challenge. Whichever methods one chooses or can afford (it can be quite expensive) certain factors are essential.

Temperature must be around 27°C (80°F) with a good humidity. The environment should be as far as possible free from cold draughts. Heliconids can stand and enjoy a very high temperature, well over 32°C (90°F). However, on hot summer days, if you are breeding in a greenhouse, some form of venting will have to be provided. Top and bottom ventilation usually lowers the temperature quickly.

Good quality foodplant is the most important factor of all. It must be provided with continuity and in sufficient quantity if a healthy colony is to be maintained.

Where you live makes a lot of difference when costing your breeding project. If your climate is mild, heating will not be too much of a problem. If you live in a colder region, heating can be very expensive.

A Breeding Colony of *Heliconius melpomone* (var. *croxstonii*)

The *croxstonii* bit is in fact a bit of fun, but I would like to write about a colony of *Heliconius melpomone* that I have at the time of writing this book. I have been breeding the colony on and off for many years and I think it should be of interest to most readers especially those interested in this particular family.

Way back in the 1970s I set up a colony of *melpomone* from a few larvae obtained from Nottingham University. The flight area was newly set up, so there were no pests to worry about; the plants and small trees flourished. It was not financially viable to breed them through the winter because of high heating costs, so each year, for several years, I would make the trip to Nottingham, cap in hand, to beg a few caterpillars or pupae or eggs to get a colony going again.

In the early 1980s it seemed unlikely that the colony at the University would be maintained for much longer; in fact, over the years it had failed several times and fresh blood had been brought in. I was also led to believe that the butterflies originated from somewhere in the Amazonian rainforests of South America. I then decided, at great expense, to try and keep them going myself at the Cotswold Wild Life Park.

Due to the demand on foodplants and problems with winter breeding, my colony deteriorated and became weak, but, at the same time, managed to hang on.

In about 1982 a young couple, Keith and Ruth Croxford, became very interested in breeding Heliconids and purchased some of my caterpillars, setting up a colony at their home. Keith is a successful businessman; successful enough to be able to holiday more or less where he chooses, and at about that time the family went to Trinidad for a couple of weeks. Whilst there they collected eggs of *Heliconius melpomone*, brought them home and released this new strain into the colony that he had purchased from me.

The Trinidad race, though the same species, are a different colour from the Amazonian race; they integrated quite freely and, because of the colour variation in the two races, practically every one was different, and so the new strain was born – hence my bit of fun – *croxstonii*.

By this time Ruth Croxford had really taken up the gauntlet and was most fascinated and dedicated with her breeding, and she devised her own personal methods, enjoying every minute of her hobby.

Through the early and mid-1980s I used to allow my colony to die out in the winter and get fresh supplies from Ruth in the spring. She was also now breeding other species, but still kept the wonderful strain of *melpomone* going.

Through 1985 to 1987 I continuously bred this strain myself, but after the winter of 1986-87 I started the new season with just *one* female. It was that year that a friend, Mr Roy Stockley, FRES, a well-known entomologist, opened a new butterfly house at Berkeley Castle in Gloucestershire. I gave him his first batch of *croxstonii* which, in his large new greenhouse, went wild; he must have bred some 4,000 individuals from 20 he took from me.

Since then, right up to the present day, he has bred between 15,000 and 20,000 butterflies at Berkeley Castle and between us we have taken *croxstonii* from strength to strength. However, the amazing fact is that *all* those thousands of butterflies came from that *one* individual that survived the winter of 1986-87. Having said this, it was Ruth Croxford who developed the strain in the early days, a strain that seems to be disease-free and disease-resistant. Her ultraclean method of breeding also kept other strains for many years until she had to give it all up after developing an allergy to the caterpillars.

THE RUTH CROXFORD METHOD

Ruth has an extension on the back of her house which measured approximately 3m (10ft) square. Inside this she set up a black nylon mesh cage of about 1.8 × 1.2m and 1.8m high (6 × 4 × 6ft). A large zip gave access, and inside were placed small potted passion flower vines for the butterflies to lay on, also various cut flowers placed in water to provide nectar and pollen. To make sure the butterflies had sufficient food, honey and water was also made available (5 per cent honey, 95 per cent water) soaked in cotton wool in coloured plastic containers. Ruth also cut discs of coloured paper and placed these on the honey-soaked cotton wool to attract the butterflies.

Super cleanliness was Ruth's secret; at all times her whole operation was spotless. Flowers and honey pads were changed every day, and the flight cage was cleaned every day. Heating was provided at approximately 27°C (80°F) by an electric heater thermostatically controlled.

Eggs were collected and surface sterilized using either Milton's baby bottle sterilizer or formaldehyde as described on pages 121–2. Milton is diluted in water using a 0.2 per cent solution and the eggs are submerged for eight minutes and then allowed to dry thoroughly. When sterilization is completed eggs are placed on a small piece of kitchen roll in a plastic box with a well-fitting lid 7.5 × 5 × 2.5cm (3 × 2 ×1in); a few *Passiflora* tendrils are also placed in the box so that newly hatched caterpillars can crawl on to them.

When 10–12 have hatched, the caterpillars are moved into a larger box, 18 × 10 × 7.5cm (7 × 4 × 3in); the move is achieved by using forceps to handle the tendrils. The batches of 10–12 caterpillars are now kept together and at no time are mixed with other batches.

Kitchen roll folded to fit the bottom of the plastic box catches frass and helps to absorb condensation. Boxes should be cleaned out *every* day even when larvae are small: though a little fiddly, this operation is quite quick and easy to do, with kitchen roll in the bottom of the box. Never place the boxes of larvae in direct sunlight.

A small amount of fresh food should be given each day, at time of cleaning only, starting with tendrils and moving on to leaves as the caterpillars grow; they should be handled as little as possible. Leaves and shoots should be handled with forceps and put into the cleaned out box with a little fresh food. Again, the secret here is a *little* fresh food.

Prior to pupation, the larvae change colour from greyish white to a pale rusty colour and begin to wander. At this stage they should be placed with great care on to a growing passion flower vine, and after some time they will hang up and pupate.

The Croxford Method has proved that it will sustain a colony for as long as you wish and this can be achieved using fewer plants than other methods. My only criticism of this method is the use of cut food. Though perfect control is achieved of the number of larvae allowed to feed, and the amount of foodplant used, the butterflies will tend to be smaller than those reared on growing plant. Also the butterflies are a little weak on emergence and take a day or so to gather their strength. This can be helped with higher temperature, but is of course, a little more costly. However, this method really does work.

Again, let me stress that the secret is cleanliness. Ruth bred the *croxstonii* strain continuously and in large numbers for about eight years using this method. If you take up this hobby and set up your own colony, you will soon realize what a wonderful achievement that was.

4. BREEDING OTHER EXOTICA

PRAYING MANTIS

There are many species of praying mantis and though their colour and size vary enormously their basic shape is the same. Some are so small they can only take small flies and insects as prey; at the other end of the scale there are giant mantis capable of taking small lizards for food.

The front legs which are immensely strong are used to catch and hold their prey while they feed; these legs are armed with needle sharp spikes set in rows. They usually impale the prey making struggling of no avail. Even large spiders are easily caught by these voracious insects.

Like all predatory animals, the mantis is meticulous in its grooming; after feeding, it cleans itself thoroughly, even moistening the legs to wipe any debris from the large compound eyes.

Once the cleaning process has started, they invariably go the whole hog, hauling their long rear legs forward, running them between the mandibles to clean them.

The mantis' name 'praying' is derived from its ever-alert stance when waiting for passing food. It holds the front 'striking' legs in a praying attitude, but when it does strike it is anything but holy, dealing death with incredible speed; in fact, the strike is between 30 and 40 micro-seconds.

To purchase and rear one mantis doesn't present many problems. It is quite easy to find enough food for one mantis, but if breeding is required there is more to it.

BREEDING INSTRUCTIONS
Individual ootheca (egg masses) are best attached to a piece of wood by means of a pin pierced through the cover of the egg case. Each is then placed in a separate closed container and kept at a temperature of 29°C (85°F). The young mantis nymphs will emerge approximately 30 days later.

Nymphs can be reared *en masse* (300–500 per ootheca)

The powerful front killing legs are rock hard and lined with sharp spikes.

When disturbed, many species adopt a threat posture to deter predators.

providing they are supplied with an excess of *Drosophila* (fruit flies) and a pad of wet cotton wool from which to drink. Both insect food and water must be replenished daily to reduce the tendency to cannibalism.

Good perches are necessary for the nymphs and these can be made out of narrow strips of balsa wood threaded on to wire mesh and attached to the roof or sides of the cage. Another good method is to stick a lot of twigs into a small flower pot filled with sand or soil; the twigs will provide plenty of places for the nymphs to sit on.

The nymphs go through five instars and at the third and fourth instar they will be large enough to feed on *Calliphora* (blow flies). These flies can be easily produced by purchasing maggots from any fishing tackle shop. The maggots are then mixed (in an escape-proof box) with an equal quantity of fine, slightly damp sawdust, and if kept at a temperature of 22°C (72°F) the maggots will pupate and the flies emerge in 12–14 days. The flies can also be kept alive for long periods by providing them with perches of rolled-up pieces of corrugated paper, a dish of wet cotton wool and lumps of sugar.

To facilitate easier handling, the flies' mobility can be greatly reduced if they are placed in the cold, at about 4°C (40°F) for half an hour before handling.

It is particularly important that the mantis nymphs are provided with good perches before they moult for the last time to become adults. At this stage the number in each cage should be reduced to allow ample room for the adults' wings to become fully inflated before they dry out.

Adult females should be isolated because at this stage they are most cannibalistic, but the males may be kept together in one cage. Adequate numbers of blow flies must be fed to both sexes daily.

Mating differs from species to species, but if the female is given a large meal and the male introduced into the female's cage while she is feeding, he will mount the female and copulation can take place while she is distracted by the food.

There are more species of mantis available now from

Second instar nymph. Its chances of becoming adult are millions to one against.

In copulation, the male and female European Praying Mantis (*Sphodromantis lineola*).

entomological dealers, but the two most popular species still seem to be the two large species *Sphodromantis lineola* and *Hierodula membranaceae*.

With *Sphodromantis* it is possible to confirm that fertilization has taken place because the empty spermataphor (sperm sac) will be found on the floor of the cage. It can be seen as a frail white empty capsule, about 2.5mm (1/10in) long. The colour slowly turns pale yellow and the capsule will crush to powder between finger and thumb.

Mantis should not be mated until they are 10–14 days old. After copulation the female must be placed in a separate cage. If the male escapes being eaten, he may be used again after two weeks.

Egg laying will commence within a few days, followed at intervals of approximately 10 days until four or six ootheca have been produced. During this period the female will have a voracious appetite and requires about 20 flies daily. If this is difficult, mantis will eat practically anything that moves, and other insects such as large moths or locusts, can be used if they are available.

Records should be kept of the date of maturation, copulation and egg laying, then infertile insects and ootheca can be discarded.

If these culture methods are followed closely, even a beginner should be able to breed most species of praying mantis.

SCORPIONS

These creatures are not my favourite animals, but it is surprising how many are transported around the world just to be kept as pets – yes, pets!

Though some of you may shudder at the very thought, the following pages are for those who find them of interest.

Scorpions have powerful stings which are brought into play as defence and sometimes to subdue prey. If the reader wishes to keep species with potentially lethal stings a Dangerous Wild Animals Licence will have to be obtained. These are issued by the Department of the Environment.

There are over 1,500 species worldwide and, though their shape is more or less constant, they vary in size from about 3cm (just over 1in) to 25cm (10in).

Like their cousins the spiders, their head and thorax is combined and is called the cephalothorax; this is broadly joined to the abdomen which consists of seven segments, followed by the very strong tail consisting of a further five segments tipped with the sting.

Scorpions have poor eyesight, even though they have between six and twelve eyes situated on the head, two in the centre and from two to five on each side. They spend the daytime hidden away under rocks and deep in burrows, venturing out to hunt for food during the hours of darkness.

Small scorpions tend to be more dangerous than larger, more powerful species. Species with weak pincers need the extra power in the tail to kill prey prior to feeding; larger scorpions rely on their powerful pincers to grab and hold, rarely using their less potent stings. However, make no mistake, every scorpion sting is very painful if not potentially dangerous.

Scorpions have eight legs each containing seven segments and tipped with a pair of tiny hooked claws. The pedipalps armed with powerful pincers make the scorpion a formidable adversary capable of subduing even the larger of its cousins the spiders.

Scorpions will eat almost anything they can catch. Various insects normally sold for feeding reptiles can be purchased from pet shops. Amongst these are crickets, locusts and mealworms. The latter are very fattening but also good food value. Cockroaches are also excellent food, but I would advise that these be crushed with forceps and placed on or near your scorpion. If not eaten, remove the corpses the next day. Other food should be given live. The only reason I suggest you kill the cockroaches is that if they escape in your house they could cause problems and be difficult to get rid of.

You may wish to breed stick insects or locusts as live food. Instructions for breeding these insects can be found on pages 154–61 and 166–8.

Scorpions need fresh water. A small dish embedded into the substrate containing cotton wool soaked with fresh water or simply filled with fresh water will be visited daily (or nightly) and this should be replenished regularly.

HOUSING YOUR SCORPIONS
Before purchasing your scorpion or scorpions make sure you learn the following details – the scientific name and country of origin; from this information you will be able to ascertain what type of habitat in terms of temperature and humidity your new pet or pets need to remain healthy.

Glass or plastic aquaria are ideal containers to house scorpions, and inside these you set up a mini-environment to suit the individual. When purchasing your container it is essential that it has, or that you make, a secure, well-fitting lid to make sure that escape is impossible.

Scorpions do not need large containers unless one intends to keep a number of individuals in one tank. If this is the case, they will need their own space; overcrowding causes fighting and deaths will occur. Ten scorpions would need a tank of approximately 1.8 × 1.2m (6 × 4ft) and to obtain these dimensions one would have to make the tank specially or have it made.

I strongly recommend that unless you are a specialist only the larger species are purchased; small scorpions are usually very fast and agile with dangerous venom. Larger scorpions are lethargic by comparison, but I must stress that they must not be handled with fingers, always use forceps of a suitable length.

So what do we put inside our tanks? How do we heat them?

Rainforest Species (hot and humid approximately 27°C (80°F))
Underheating is most suitable for these species and this can be maintained with a heating pad placed under the tank. Various materials can be used as a substrate – sand, peat, soil or bark chippings. However, sand will tend to become dry very quickly and problems can occur with mites and other pests using peat or bark chippings. By far the best material for these species is vermiculite, an inert material which is used with compost for pot plants.

Vermiculite retains moisture for long periods and is a perfect base to create the humidity your captives need. Your nearest garden centre should be able to supply this inexpensive substrate for your tank, which should be placed to a depth of 7.5cm (3in).

Scorpions like to be able to hide, so rocks and pieces of bark, which will also serve as decoration, should be placed in the tank. Spray daily to maintain a high level of humidity.

Species recommended for this environment are *Heterometrus longimannus* from the Philippines, *Heterometrus fulvipes* from Malaysia and *Pandinus imperater* from Africa.

Desert Species (hot and dry 27°C (80°F))
The substrate is very important for desert scorpions. I would suggest 2.5cm (1in) of washed and thoroughly dried gravel topped by 7.5cm (3in) of sharp sand; it is very important to keep the substrate clean and bone dry. Drinking water should be provided but care should be taken that water does not overflow into the sand.

Various pieces of rock and bark can be placed into the sand

for hiding places and a heating pad should again be used to heat the tank from underneath.

Several species are suitable for desert tanks. *Leiurus quinquestriatus* is from the Middle East; this species has a sting that could prove fatal. *Androctonus australis* is from north Africa; this species is very agile and quick to use its sting, which again can prove fatal. *Buthus occitanus* is also from the Middle East and is another species with a very potent sting. *Scorpio maurus* is from Israel and is a good species for the beginner; as with all scorpions, the sting is painful but no reported deaths have occurred with this species.

Temperature Species (room temperature)
Most European species do well in the temperate tank. Providing they are kept at living-room temperature, no heating is necessary. Substrate is not so important, though I would recommend that one side of the tank be kept slightly moist, so vermiculite would best suit; and the other side could be gravel and/or sand. Again, provide plenty of hiding places with stones and bark.

The information that has been offered here for the purpose of keeping scorpions has only scratched the surface of this interesting hobby. If you wish to keep one scorpion of a species that is not potentially dangerous, then the information contained here is adequate; however, if you want to develop your hobby, I would suggest a separate and comprehensive book is needed. Remember some scorpions can be lethal if not treated with the utmost respect.

STICK INSECTS

I am not going to describe in endless detail various species of these fascinating insects; I will say, however, that stick insects or Phasmids are comparatively easy to keep and easy to breed providing certain ground rules are observed.

Up until about 10 years ago, the mention of stick insects would conjure up the good old laboratory species, *Carausius morosus*, from India. This small species, fed on privet or ivy, has been kept in schools and universities for many years. However, interest has grown, and when one considers that there are approximately 2,500 species worldwide, with the largest attaining lengths of about 35cm (14in) (!) one begins to understand why there is even a Phasmid Society in which members 'swap' specimens and newly attained knowledge about the well-being of their creatures. Consequently, no self-respecting insect breeding book should fail to mention stick insects, and the following are what I consider to be the few most widely kept members of this family with the deliberate exclusion of good old *Carausius morosus*.

Giant Spiny Stick Insect
Extatosoma tiaratum
I first came face to face with a large female *tiaratum* in 1972, and I marvelled as its size and strength.

FOOD PLANTS
These bizarre creatures are native to Papua New Guinea and northern Australia and in their wild state one of the foodplants on which they feed is the leaf of the sago palm tree. It is said that at certain times of the year, when the females are laying eggs, it is almost like rain spattering down from the palms.

The sago palm has a thick central stem with small leaves

growing from each side giving the appearance of one large leaf. Wind damage often breaks many of these small leaves which curl up and turn brown. Female *Extatosoma tiaratum*, motionless, hanging in the trees, look very much like these damaged leaves which afford them excellent camouflage.

For captive breeding bramble is, in my opinion, the best foodplant because it can be obtained all the year round; however, they will also take rose and oak.

The foodplant should be kept with the stems in water, but ensure that nymphs cannot get into the water and drown. Whatever foodplant you may choose, it is, of course, not the correct one. Plants which these insects feed on in the wild will not be available in the United Kingdom or North America. Though many nymphs take readily to their substitute food, others may need a little persuasion; cutting away the leaf edges leaving a raw edge may help. Even with the best will in the world some will fail to feed and die.

Breeding instructions

E. tiaratum can be purchased as ova or nymphs (young immature insects), but I will start with the egg; they are greyish in colour streaked with buff and have a small knob (capitulum) protruding at one end. Eggs should be incubated at approximately 24°C (75°F) and will take between six and ten months to hatch. During this period they must be kept moist; thus a good form of successful incubation is obtained by placing the eggs on moist silver sand inside a perspex or plastic box. The box should have a tight fitting lid and care should be taken to ensure that during their long incubation period they are not allowed to become dry.

Because the eggs take such a long time to hatch it may be preferred, initially, to buy nymphs.

On hatching, the nymphs are about 12mm (½in) in length and very dark brown, indeed, almost black except for a pale yellowish collar tinted red. They are quite active at this stage and will run as soon as the lid is taken off the incubating box. In the wild they move up into the trees to search for food and the numbers eaten by predators must be staggering.

Any kind of container or cage is suitable to keep them in and a particularly successful cage is described on pages 160–1. At all times they must be in a humid atmosphere; this can be obtained by thoroughly spraying the foodplant at least once, and preferably twice, each day with tepid water.

At all times keep the rearing cage at a temperature above 20°C (68°F); below this the insects will be sluggish and if the temperature is constantly low they will die.

Over the following four to five months the nymphs will progress through five instars, and each time a skin is shed the insect will almost double in size. After the first of these changes the insects lose their dark colour, turning sandy brown. Even at this early stage the sexes can be easily distinguished. The females are slightly larger and thicker than the males, they also have soft spikes on the abdomen and are a brighter sandy brown; leaf-like projections on the abdomen are also in evidence. The males are paler in colour, more of a greyish yellow and their abdomens are smooth by comparison with the females.

From this period onwards colour in both sexes will depend on the degree of humidity given to their cage. If spraying is repeated frequently, several times each day, the adults are often pale green. However, if there is insufficient spraying both nymphs and adults take on a duller darker appearance.

To observe a skin change is a fascinating experience. The insect hangs upside down from a bramble stem and after several hours begins to strain with rhythmical convulsions. Eventually, the top of the thorax splits just behind the head and the fresh insect slowly emerges straining to free itself with considerable effort. Half emerged, it is as large as the old skin; one wonders how the old skin could possibly have contained so much. Once the head, thorax and legs are free, the insect rests suspended for about 30 minutes; after this time it reaches upwards, gains a hold, and the abdomen finally slips free. It takes several hours for the fresh insect to regain its strength and 'harden off'. During this time movement is infrequent and feeble. Its first meal is often its old skin; nothing in nature seems to be wasted.

By the fourth instar, the females are considerably larger than males. The legs of both sexes are extremely hard and armed with short sharp spikes. The female's abdomen is fat and round, the male's thin and smooth. At this stage the female is approximately 13cm (5in) long and the male 9cm (3½in).

Finally, adults will begin to appear; a good sized female now measures about 17.5cm (7in) and the legs are hard and powerful. If roughly handled they will snap the rear legs over unsuspecting fingers – human blood can be spilled.

The bulky females now find it impossible to walk upright and are forced by their weight to hang upside down. I was surprised to discover how little they eat compared with other large insects. The females are also flightless, only possessing rudimentary wing cases which are never unfolded.

The male is much smaller, 12.5cm (5in) in length, and much lighter bodied. Their wings are fully developed and they will fly from tree to tree in search of females or when disturbed. The wings are quite beautiful, multi-pleated, folding into narrow strips when not in use. They are semi-transparent with greyish black markings and covered with sandy brown protective wing cases.

EXTATOSOMA TIARATUM USED AS FOOD

In Papua New Guinea, the leaves of the sago palm, which constitutes the main food plant of the Giant Spiny Stick Insect, also make good roof thatching material. The people of this region live in large family groups, five to ten families in one house, which is called a 'long house'. The houses are built on piles or stilts because of the rainforest conditions, and several times a year the roofs have to be rethatched.

The women prepare a thatching feast and the men move off into the rain forest to collect large bundles of sago palm leaves. On their return, the leaves are cleaned up, dead leaves are brushed out, and at this stage many Giant Spiny Stick Insects are usually found and promptly handed over to the women for cooking. They are skewered with fine-pointed sticks pushed from the abdomen tip up through the head and spit roasted over an open fire until the legs fall off; at this stage they are ready to eat. The flesh of these large insects is pink in colour, in fact, very meaty-looking, but what it tastes like I can only guess. I have actually seen this thatching feast on film which was taken about 20 years ago. The natives also ate large spiders cooked in the same way. Whether this practice still exists today I do not know.

Queensland Titan
Acrophylla wulfingi
The female *A. wulfingi* does not have the bulk of *Extatosoma tiaratum* but is, nevertheless, just as impressive, being much longer. A good sized female can measure up to 25cm (10in), though the male is much smaller and thinner.

Wings of both sexes are well developed and the male can fly. The female is much too heavy for flight, but could flutter downwards if disturbed.

Breeding instructions for this species are the same as for *E. tiaratum*, but *A. wulfingi* do not like as much humidity; one light spray with tepid water daily is all that is required. The eggs are only about half the size of *tiaratum* and very dark brown, appearing black in colour; the gestation period is again over six months.

The nymphs are 2–2.5cm (about 1in) long on hatching, and one wonders how they could have come from such small eggs. They are mainly bright green in colour and a little more difficult to start feeding. Bramble is again my recommendation, though they will take rose and oak, and trimming the leaf edges will often entice them to feed. I have found over-watering can cause fatalities, even at third instar, so be careful not to overdo the spraying.

The following species can also be cultured using the *tiaratum* method.
Eurycantha calcarata from Indonesia
Clitumnus extradentatus (Thorny Stick)
Dixippus morosus (Indian Stick) on privet or ivy
Carausius morosus

Necrosia sipylus (Pink-winged Stick) – this species is straw coloured and parthenogenic (no male needed), with pink lacy wings. Unlike many other species the gestation period is only six weeks. The eggs are affixed to the foodplant with a natural gum; the nymphs are bright green on hatching and take readily to bramble. Pink-winged Sticks are very easy and I recommend them as a starter for the beginner.

Jungle Nymph
Heteropteryx dilatata
This massive stick insect is a most impressive creature to say the very least. Females are normally bright green but occasionally golden in colour and completely covered by an awesome array of spines. All the legs are rock hard, and great care should be taken when they are handled. They will snap the rear legs over fingers and hold tight as blood drips from spike wounds.

They can be bred using the same breeding method as described for *Extatosoma tiaratum* and I would say they are easier, providing the sprayer is used liberally.

The only way this stick differs in its breeding habits is in the way it deposits its eggs. *Heteropteryx dilatata* is native to central Malaya and when the female is ready to commence egg laying she does so under the cover of darkness. She descends from the trees or shrubs to the ground, plunges her sharp pointed ovipositor into the ground and lays her eggs in small batches. It is the delicate nature of the eggshell that requires this method of laying. The eggs need the protection of the soil to prevent damage. The eggs are best kept in damp peat at a temperature of 23°C (74°F). Though they can begin hatching after about 10 months, don't throw them away after a year, because they can go as long as 16 months and still hatch.

The males are not nearly as impressive as the females, being a mottled brown colour and very similar to a male *Extatosoma tiaratum*. Females are also brown until at least the fourth instar when they attain their brilliant green coloration.

The male has fully developed wings capable of flight, but

the female has only very small wings that are pale pink in colour, and hidden under hard green wing cases. It is with the pink wings that there hangs a tale of great interest. Even with their great size (a female can measure up to about 20cm (8in)), when in the comparative safety of a tree, amongst green leaves, these insects are very well camouflaged. It is when they descend to the ground to lay their eggs that they become vulnerable to attack from insectivorous predators. The rainforest canopy starves the ground of light so that little greenery can survive at ground level and the general appearance of the forest floor is dull and lifeless. Here the large green female is no longer protected by camouflage, in fact she is now rather conspicuous. However, she has quite a trick up her sleeve. If approached by a predator she rears up on tiptoe and extends her rear legs into a horizontal splayed position. At the same time, she opens her tiny wing cases, and vibrates them, making a distinct hissing sound. The pink underwings are now fully visible and if the attacker persists, she will snap her very strong rear legs shut over the nearest appendage that comes her way.

When a snake strikes the mouth is opened revealing a pink interior. In dim light on the jungle floor I am sure a predator could mistake this defensive female for a snake; the speed at which she snaps her rear legs at her attacker would appear like the strike of a snake. This is all pure conjecture on my part, but I am convinced that this strange defensive behaviour has sent many a would-be predator packing, leaving the stick insect to lay her eggs another day.

A Cage for Housing Stick Insects

The following is a method of housing all the stick insects mentioned, and is particularly successful with *Extatosoma tiaratum* and *Heteropteryx dilatata*.

A large wooden, solid sided, and glass fronted cage is made with a wooden flap at the rear taking up least one half of the back of the cage from the centre to the base. The cage should measure at least 1 × 1 × 0.3m (3 × 3 × 1ft) and in the base should be placed a tray taking up the whole floor area and at least 10cm (4in) deep, filled with moist peat. The top should be made of perforated aluminium on a wooden frame and some form of under heating should be provided to achieve a constant temperature of 23°C (74°F).

Large quantities of bramble can be placed in a tank of this size in at least two containers holding water to keep the foodplants fresh. Bramble will usually last at least a week and it should be well sprayed with tepid water at least once a day. Spraying keeps the peat base well moist and *Extatosoma tiaratum* eggs will fall on to the peat where they will remain until the nymphs hatch with no other attention.

Female *Heteropteryx dilatata* will descend to the peat base usually at night, and deposit their eggs directly into the peat where they will remain, with no further attention, until they hatch.

I have tried this method for the last two years and it has worked very well indeed. At the time of writing, my large cage contains over 80 nymphs of *Heteropteryx dilatata* all of which have hatched from the peat base, and each time the bramble is changed the numbers grow.

LEAF INSECTS

Javanese Leaf Insect
Phyllium crucifolium

This truly incredible insect belongs to the subfamily *Pseudophasmatinae* and its leaf-like camouflage is quite extraordinary. Both the male and female imago (adult) are winged, and although the female rarely flies the male has a well-controlled, even delicate flight.

The male imago is 5–6.5cm (2–2½in) long, the abdomen is paper thin and just under 2.5cm (1in) wide. The lace-like wings are multi-pleated, folding neatly down the centre of the thorax and abdomen in a narrow strip. Even the legs are like small leaves, apparently growing from the base of a larger one. The topside of the insect is greyish green, the underside a definite green, but darker and vein-like lines also add to the leaf-like camouflaged appearance.

The female is much larger and thicker, 7.5–8.5cm (3–3½ in) in length and almost 5cm (2in) wide. Like other Phasmidae (stick insects, leaf insects, etc.) they will often sway from side to side when disturbed, mimicking a leaf gently moving in a light breeze.

BREEDING INSTRUCTIONS

The breeder of this fascinating species is faced with only one major problem – getting the newly hatched nymphs to feed. The natural foodplant is possibly guava, although this is impossible for most breeders. Bramble, again, makes a successful substitute, as do oak and evergreen oak. If the breeder is only able to breed enough to keep the stock going, this is a satisfactory result.

One female will produce about 40 eggs, at a rate of one or two a day. They are spherical, deeply ridged with an indentation at one end. Inside the indentation is a small protruding projection like a tiny cork; this is called the

Even the legs of the leaf insect look like small leaves.

capitulum and it is pushed out when hatching. The general appearance of the egg is that of a seed, and the colour is very dark brown. The eggs should be placed on moist silver sand in a plastic or perspex box. The box should have a tightly fitting lid and the temperature for incubation should be 20–25°C (68–77°F).

On hatching, the nymphs are dark reddish brown and this is the crucial period for the breeder. A larger perspex or glass container or a medium sized seed propagator is most suitable for housing the nymphs, and mature bramble, not tender young shoots (if bramble is used) is the more favoured food. The foodplant should be placed in a container of fresh water, but great care should be taken to ensure that your nymphs cannot fall into the water. It is advisable to place the foodplant so that leaves touch the sides and top of your container so that if nymphs walk off the foodplant the chances are that they will find it again. Cut the edges away from the leaves to give a raw edge; this often tempts nymphs to feed. Keep the leaves wet by spraying with tepid water two or three times daily and place the container in a light but not sunny position where the temperature will not fall below 20°C (68°F) even at night.

All the nymphs will be seen drinking water from the wet leaves, and this will encourage some of them to begin feeding. Those that do will quickly lose their dark colour and turn pale green, the rest will die after a few days. I have learned from breeding this species that greater numbers always lead to a larger percentage starting to feed, as though they trigger each other into feeding. The greatest success that I ever achieved with leaf insects was at my first exhibition at Bourton-on-the-Water. I placed a couple of dozen nymphs of Giant Spiny Stick Insects, *Extatosoma tiaratum*, in with the tiny leaf insects, and they seemed to trigger off the latter to feed. I ended up with a wonderful colony of about 50 adults.

I emulated this success after moving to the Cotswold Wild Life Park but decided after a couple of years not to exhibit them because no matter how successful, visitors to my exhibition were forever asking what was on display in the tank. They were so well camouflaged people just could not see them.

Males tend to mature more quickly and will often attempt to mate with immature females. When a female reaches maturity she usually mates within 24 hours.

Javanese Leaf Insects must be rated as one of the most fascinating and rewarding insects to breed. They are quite harmless and odourless. If you must handle them, coax them very gently to walk on to the hand, as they will easily shed a leg if handled roughly. Treat them with great care.

LOCUSTS

Though locusts are bred in many universities throughout the world and used in research work of many kinds, many are bred just to be used as a source of food for pets – lizards, spiders, scorpions, etc. Locusts have been known as a scourge of man since Biblical times, ravaging crops causing famine and death. Man has also been a scourge to the locusts, trying to wipe them from the face of the earth and breeding them as food for other creatures, even eating them himself.

Records of swarm movement and size have been kept for years, and in the year 1889 the largest swarm ever recorded manifested itself in the vicinity of the Red Sea. Scientists of the day estimated that the swarm of *Schistocerca gregaria*, the Desert Locust, contained approximately 250 billion individuals weighing about 500,000 tons. When one considers that a locust can eat its own weight in a day, that is an awful lot of greenery. Thinking on that kind of scale, it is little wonder that we have tried and tried to exterminate them from the face of the earth, but without success.

There are two species widely bred, one is the above-mentioned Desert Locust, the other is *Locusta migratoria*, the Migratory Locust. There are several subspecies of *Schistocerca* to be found in the Americas and entomologists have wondered for years whether or not the American forms originated from *gregaria*, but could not be sure how they managed to get across the sea. In 1988 a considerable swarm arrived in Trinidad having flown 5,000 kilometres (3,000 miles) across the Atlantic Ocean; no mean feat for an insect. The scientists are now pretty sure that it had been done before, and that the American form could have evolved in this way.

BREEDING INSTRUCTIONS
I have no need to dwell too long on this subject; a few ground rules have to be observed to ensure successful breeding. It all

This locust hopper will soon be on the wing. Just one skin change to go. The species seen here is *Schistocerca gregaria*, the Desert Locust.

The Desert Locust is known to have flown non-stop 5,000 kilometres (3,000 miles) across the Atlantic Ocean.

depends on how many are needed to meet your requirements.

Locusts can be bred in dust bins, wooden containers, glass containers – just about any kind of container can be used. They need a temperature in some part of their tank to be approximately 36°C (97°F) and this is achieved by one, two or three (depending on tank size) naked 60 watt lamp bulbs fitted inside the container. Plenty of perches must be provided for the hoppers (young) to hang on to when they shed their skins through five instars. Frass and uneaten food should be cleaned out daily and most cultures are fed on grass or cabbage; I feed my colony on cabbage.

Females lay their eggs in slightly moist sand which can be provided in any kind of container providing it is at least 10cm (4in) deep and large enough for the female to gain access. The female has a natural digging mechanism which turns her whole abdomen into an ovipositor. She bores a hole approximately 10cm (4in) deep and deposits approximately 100 eggs in the bottom. As she withdraws her abdomen she produces a water-absorbing foam which protects the eggs and prevents them from drying out.

Once egg laying has been observed, the sand container can be left in the tank, or removed and placed in another container to await hatching. This can vary slightly depending on temperature, but keep the sand damp with light sprayings of tepid water; hoppers should appear within 10–14 days. The first thing the hatchling does is to shed its skin, then the continuous process of eating and growing begins. The complete life cycle takes from four to six weeks depending on temperature and after each hatch the cage should be thoroughly cleaned, the egg-laying container cleaned and the sand replaced. Providing these simple rules are followed, your breeding containers can be as simple or sophisticated, large or small, as you wish, and success is assured.

LARGE SPIDERS

Keeping large spiders or tarantulas as pets is a hobby that has grown from virtually nothing 20 years ago to the present day when it is very popular. When John Midwinter and I opened our Butterfly and Invertebrate Exhibition in the early 1970s we were very fortunate to obtain two large spiders from a friend who had actually imported them himself. Today, many pet shops carry stocks of large spiders and some dealers import them 5,000 at a time.

Personally, I am concerned for the continued well-being of some of these beautiful creatures. The Rusty-kneed Tarantula (*Brachypelma smithi*) has been hounded almost to extinction by collectors (for profit), and is now an endangered species as a direct result. To replace it in the spider market another species has now come 'on song'. They are calling this one the True Red-legged Tarantula (*Brachypelma emilia*); now these are being imported in thousands. How long before it too is scarce or even endangered through over-collecting? I do not want to sound like a kill-joy, but *emilia*, though quite placid in temperament, has a very toxic bite. In most pet shops you would not be told this, largely because the owners won't even know.

I am not an arachnologist and I have only added spiders to my book for one reason – in the hope that those that are purchased will be looked after properly and therefore live longer, reducing the market for wild-collected spiders, and perhaps increasing home-bred ones. Twenty years ago very few people kept spiders. Since then literally millions have been collected for the pet trade. Most of these spiders have been collected over the past 10 years, and most of the species have a life span of over 10 years. Where are they today? All those millions of spiders, especially the millions of Rusty-kneed Tarantulas, are mostly dead because they were not cared for or fed properly.

I suppose I should shoulder some of the blame myself because I have exhibited large spiders in my invertebrate houses over the years; this must have induced many people into keeping a spider. I have also sold the odd specimen when I have been asked to procure them for my own customers.

HOUSING YOUR SPIDERS

Contrary to what many will recommend, large spiders do not need or enjoy large tanks to live in. Space makes them insecure; a container 30 × 25cm and 30cm high (12 × 10 × 12in) is quite adequate for most large spiders. The tank can be made of plastic, perspex or glass, or tailor made out of wood with a glass front for observation. One thing is a must; make sure that it is escape proof. The most suitable substrate is a material called vermiculite, which I mentioned when writing about scorpions, and this can be obtained from garden centres. Vermiculite is a totally inert substance; it holds moisture and creates a pleasant humid atmosphere. It is also an excellent medium for burrowing into, which many spiders enjoy. Place 7.5–10cm (3–4in) of substrate in your 'spider house', having soaked it in water and the excess squeezed out beforehand.

Your spider will need a retreat, a place to hide away if it wishes, a place where it can feel safe and secure. This can be provided in the shape of a half-buried flower pot of suitable size; two-thirds of a coconut shell with the meat removed looks good and does the job. A large flat smooth stone placed next to the retreat makes a suitable resting place which will also be used by your captive on occasions. Other bits and pieces like cork bark are also useful and double as tank decoration.

I would recommend one of three methods for heating your spider house. Whichever you choose, it will need to be on a thermostat of good quality that will hold the temperature without much fluctuation; a thermometer should also be placed inside your tank so that you can ensure that the correct temperature is maintained.

Method one is the use of light bulbs mounted above the tank. These should be inside a box or false lid; the spiders should not be able to make direct contact, or they will be burnt. If light bulbs are used they must be red or blue; spiders cannot see these colours. White light will irritate your spider and make it insecure.

Method two is underheating with a heat pad, as used in seed propagators. If this method is adopted, careful checks should be made regularly to ensure the correct temperature is being maintained. If a spider is too warm, it will burrow down to escape the heat. If underheating became too warm the unfortunate creature would burrow down to even greater heat and this could have fatal results.

Finally in method three, if several spiders are being kept the tanks can all be placed on a shallow box construction containing a tubular greenhouse heater. These heaters are about 60 watts per 30cm (12in); holes can be cut in the top of the box to allow heat to the base of your tanks. Again, regular checks on temperature are essential; it is better to be slightly under temperature than over.

Large species eat large meals – ideal food is live food – locusts, crickets, mealworms, moths, grasshoppers, stick insects (but only small species), some beetles. If it moves try it, your spider will discard it if it is not to its liking. A happy spider will feed – if it will not feed conditions are not correct. All the large spiders are natives of the tropics and sub-tropics. Temperature should be at least 23°C (74°F) and humidity should be 80 per cent. If your spider will not feed and it is not about to moult raise the temperature by two or three degrees but do not exceed 25°C (77°F).

Place a few large clumps of sphagnum moss into the tank and raise the humidity by spraying the substrate – heat and humidity will be the key – juggle the two until you get it right, and once you have, all will be well. Don't buy a spider unless you know what species it is and where it comes from, this will give you a good guide as to the correct temperature and humidity it needs; having said this even individuals of the same species can vary in their likes and dislikes.

HANDLING LARGE SPIDERS

Spider books seem to elaborate on whether or not the spider keeper should handle the pet spider or not. My views on this subject are – do not handle any large spider. It is not at all a natural thing to do, it invariably worries the spider and is a prime cause of hair shedding. What is hair shedding? This is a natural defence mechanism whereby the spider vibrates its rear legs across the abdomen sending clouds of abdominal hair into the air. If this shed hair gets into the eyes or on to delicate skin it can cause severe irritation and with some species permanent damage to fingers and so on. The hair does not carry any chemical irritants but it has minute barbed ends that automatically bore into skin. If sufficient numbers find their way into a finger joint, this is when real damage can occur. So, I know it may be tempting; I handle my spiders on occasions, but my advice is don't handle them at all.

MOULTING

The spider's skin is tough and hard; as with insects, it acts as a skeleton, and is in fact called an exoskeleton. A creature with an exoskeleton cannot enlarge itself so, in order to grow, it has to shed its skin revealing a new larger one underneath. Spiderlings shed several times a year because they are growing fast; adult females moult about once a year but adult males only live nine months or so and during this time they do not moult at all.

Some spiders tend to shed large quantities of hair from the abdomen prior to skin changing, leaving a bald patch. If the skin of your spider is pale in colour, and most of them are, the bald patch will give you a good indication that the spider is about to moult. The patch will turn darker, almost black, a few days prior to the moult. This coloration is caused by the hair on the new skin showing through the old one.

If you do become aware that moulting is imminent remove any live food that may be in your tank. After moulting, whilst the new skin and fangs are soft, spiders are very vulnerable. I once lost a beautiful Mexican Red Rump (*Brachypelma vagans*) when a cricket began eating it as it moulted and the unfortunate spider bled to death.

Some species web themselves up in an elaborate cocoon prior to moulting, but most species simply spin a carpet of silk across an indentation in the substrate and moult on that. A few species, *Brachypelma smithi* to name one, lie on their backs prior to moulting. Whichever way it happens, it is a crucial time for the spider. If conditions are not good, deaths can occur. If you are aware that a skin change is imminent, make sure that temperature and humidity are perfect.

Never assist your pet. It is a painfully slow process, but one that has been going on for millions of years; they have perfected their methods and you will not improve on them.

All spiders moult in the same way. The skin splits around the base of the carapace (top of the cephalothorax), which falls away in one piece. The fresh spider slowly eases itself out of the opening, pushing the old skin away; the skin of the abdomen usually peels off in two or three strips. The whole process lasts about an hour, but it can take longer. If you have a spider that has shed a leg for some reason, after its skin change you will find that the leg has been replaced. However, it will not be full size, probably about 60 per cent of the size of its opposite leg; it takes several skin changes to attain its original length and colour.

BREEDING INSTRUCTIONS

If we are to curb over-collecting, one way that could certainly help would be captive breeding. Having said this, one would never make a living breeding large spiders, it would have to be done for love and not for profit. My own limited attempts to breed them have not met with any success, but then I would have to admit that I am not an arachnologist; I have only ever possessed a couple of males over the years. Several of my professional friends have bred *Avicularia avicularia* (the Pink Toe) also *Psalmopoeus cambridgei* (the Chevron), both from Trinidad.

The males I have had, on two occasions, were both *Brachypelma smithi* (the Rusty-kneed Tarantula); each time I had them as immatures, each time I observed the fresh adult build a 'sperm web', crawl underneath and produce a white patch of sperm, then clamber back on top of the web and fill their palpal bulbs. Each time the male has mated with all my females and several belonging to friends, but only once did a female produce eggs. That particular female (which was positively huge and only had six legs), belonged to a friend, who shall remain nameless. He was really thrilled and rang me to pass on the good news. About a month later he decided to have a close look at the egg-sac and picked it up. The next morning the female had eaten it and all the eggs were gone.

I was furious and told him that I thought his action had most likely prompted her to eat the egg-sac, but he didn't agree. I am still convinced that I lost my one chance to be able to say 'I have bred Rusty-kneed Tarantulas' because the eggs were handled. It must be common sense *not* to touch.

Getting spiders to mate or, to rephrase, getting the male to fertilize the female is not difficult and there are several ways to go about it. If the female's living container is large enough, simply place the male in with her, but if you have taken my advice, she will not be in a large container; so remove her and put her in a tank with just a dry substrate of sand at least 60 × 30cm and 30cm high (2 × 1 × 1ft). Introduce the male about 10 minutes later.

Another method is to introduce them to each other in the centre of a large low coffee table covered with a tablecloth or even on the floor. Wherever they are introduced you then stay with them until it is all over; the whole business can take just a few minutes or quite some time to happen.

The male will approach the female and begin very lightly and spasmodically to drum his long front legs. Eventually the tips of his toes will touch the female and whichever direction she is facing she will usually turn to face him. The male may continue his excited spasmodic drumming for some time, as though he is testing for any signs of aggression; eventually he will make his move. He brings his front legs together at the tips and works them between the female's front legs. Just above the second leg joint the male has a tiny spur or tibial hook; he uses these hooks to trap the female's fangs, which

The Pink-toe from Trinidad (*Avicularia avicularia*) makes a nest about 3m (10ft) from the ground on the trunk of the tonka-bean tree.

Another Trinidad species, *Psalmopeous cambridgei*, the Chevron, is not an easy species to handle.

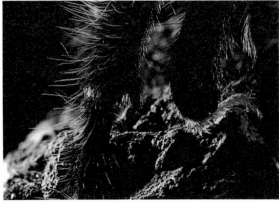

The male Rusty-kneed Tarantula, left, locks the female's fangs with tibial hooks situated just above the second joint of his front legs.

The tiny spurs or tibial hooks, above the second joint of the male spider's front legs, are used to lock the female's fangs when mating.

by this time are drawn for action. He then bends the female over backwards stretching out his palps, searching for the genital slit (the epigyne) on the underside of the female's abdomen.

Once the male has found his mark, he will leave the female immediately, as by this time she may have become aggressive. If left in a cage the male could become a large meal, so get him out of harm's way as quickly as possible. You now begin the long wait to see if the mating was successful.

It will be several months before eggs are produced, depending on the species, but if you are fortunate and your female does produce, she is likely to become aggressive and should be disturbed as little as possible. It is very important to ensure that conditions are perfect whilst she has her eggs. She will move the egg-sac about her tank placing it where she feels it should be – closer to heat or moisture, for example. If she becomes agitated through bad conditions she may well eat her eggs. However, let's be optimistic; you do everything correctly and your eggs hatch. Leave the spiderlings with the female for six to eight weeks, then separate the whole brood into small containers on vermiculite. Before and after separation, give the spiderlings plenty of food, making sure that the vermiculite in their small containers is kept damp. The rest is dedication and perhaps a little luck.

So now you think, perhaps, it may be fun to keep a tarantula. The problem you face is, should you or should you not encourage the over-collecting and subsequent endangerment of them by doing so? I can only suggest that you remember that *smithi* is now an endangered species as a direct result of being every spider keeper's favourite. If you must have one, only buy from a dealer who knows what he is talking about and can give you all the information as to origin and wild conditions. Better still, try and purchase a spiderling that has been bred by an expert. You can then pick his brains and make sure that it has the best possible chance of growing up. With the breeder's knowledge and what you have learned here, perhaps it will.

LEAF CUTTERS – FUNGUS-GROWING ANTS

The leaf-cutting ants of the New World belong to the tribe the Attini, within the subfamily Myrmicinae, and take in 190 species. They comprise three groups, namely, the primitive, transitional and advanced genera. It is the latter, consisting of 24 species of *Acromyrmex* and 15 species of *Atta*, that create the most impact everywhere that they occur.

These ants cut leaves in order to produce a substrate on which they cultivate a species of fungus. The ants eat only the fungus that they cultivate, and the fungus is only to be found inside the ants' nests. If the ants are removed from the fungus, it is quickly overrun by competing species of fungi

The fungus garden is at the very heart of the ant colony. Seen here is the species *Acromyrmex octospinosus*.

and other organisms; it is unable to compete on its own without the attention of the ants. If the ants are removed from their fungus gardens, they too soon succumb and die of starvation. This truly remarkable symbiotic relationship between an insect and a plant is one that has created great interest and study in the scientific world.

How does it work? The ants produce fungus gardens in the substrate, and within these gardens live the single queen and brood (larvae) as well as, in some species, millions of workers. Not all members of the Myrmicinae cut leaves to aid the culture of fungus. The primitive genera, which produce the smallest colonies (some consisting of fewer than 100 individuals), grow their fungus on particles of dead vegetal matter and insect excrement.

The transitional genera, such as *Trachymyrmex* and *Sericomyrmex*, cut leaves and flowers, but their colonies attain proportions of only about 700 to 1,000 individuals.

Acromyrmex reach colony sizes of 10,000 to 20,000 and create one large fungus garden or three or four smaller ones. But it is *Atta* which produce gigantic nests that may cover and dominate a ground area of over 100 square metres (120 square yards) with excavations to a depth of 2m (more than 6ft). These nests contains up to 400 separate fungus gardens containing up to 7 million ants, depending on the species.

The *Atta* species usually obtained for exhibition and study purposes is *Atta cephalotes* from Trinidad. Their nests in the wild reach maximum numbers of about 700,000 containing about 80 fungus gardens.

Not all the underground chambers excavated by the ants contain active gardens; some are used as rubbish tips for spent fungus garden debris and dead ants, though both *Atta* and *Acromyrmex* will often trail up low shrubs and drop their refuse from the tip of a branch. When this happens, the piles of refuse can get quite large.

At an American university a young and vigorous colony of *Atta cephalotes* was maintained under carefully controlled laboratory conditions. During the course of a year the ants established two fungus gardens, using over 2kg (4½lb) of freshly cut leaves in the process. The gardens measured about 1,200 cubic centimetres (75 cubic inches). Many gardens in nature would have twice this bulk and take twice this weight of leaf to complete.

How are the gardens actually propagated? Cut leaf sections are brought into the nest and are then cut into smaller pieces, about a millimetre or two in diameter. During this process, the pieces are moistened by the mouth parts of the ants. The edges of the leaf are now pressed by the mandibles so that they become wet and pulpy, and at this stage the worker ant deposits a clear anal droplet which contains a powerful enzyme complex to speed the breakdown of the substrate. The leaf is then incorporated into the garden and from time to time tufts of fungal mycelium are placed on to the new medium to grow.

On this base the fungus grows and produces masses of hyphal swellings (gongylidia), which is the highly nutritious part of the fungus eaten by the ants and fed to the queen and the brood.

The fungus also produces detoxification enzymes which neutralize any harmful material produced either in the leaf or as the substrate ferments. An example of these harmful substances are tannins and other phenolic compounds that are produced by trees and shrubs to protect themselves against insect attack, usually by caterpillars. The tannins would suppress or even kill caterpillars, but are rendered harmless to the ants by the detoxification enzymes produced by the fungus. It has been found that laboratory colonies of these ants can even utilize laurel leaves which produce prussic acid that is normally lethal to insects. The fungus renders the fermenting laurel leaves harmless to the ants.

So the ants create a perfect medium on which many species of fungus can flourish. We have established that the ant fungus is weak and cannot survive alone, so, how does it compete when millions of alien spores must be accidentally carried into the nest by the foraging workers? The answer proved to be yet another fascinating discovery. Each ant is able to secrete a chemical called hydroxydecanoic acid

Stems as well as leaves
are used in the fungus
gardens.

Smooth leaves are
preferred to hairy ones.

Even leaves as thick as cabbage are not a problem. The workers can carry about five times their body weight.

(myrmicacin) from a gland in the thorax (the metathoracic gland); this chemical suppresses and kills fungal spores. The ants' fungus, which is now widely known as *Attamyces bromatificus*, is not affected by this chemical, because it is cultivated by the ants from tufts or mycelium (cuttings if you like), and does not produce any spores.

The ant fungus varies from species to species in the amount of gongylidia produced. The species producing the largest colonies also grow the most productive fungus. Compare *Atta cephalotes* from Trinidad with *Atta sexdens rubropilosa* from Paraguay. The latter fungus is almost four times more productive than that of *cephalotes* and this is reflected in colony size; *cephalotes* produces approximately 700,000 and *rubropilosa* 3,000,000 individuals.

Each year after the first rains many thousands of winged males and females (gyne) leave the parent colonies and proceed on their nuptial flights. Females may mate with several males before descending to attempt the founding of a

The workers touch antenna when passing just to make sure they are sisters. If they are not, fighting would be the immediate reaction.

new colony. Males soon die, but the females shed their wings and labour for six to eight hours excavating their first tunnel and a small brood chamber. The vast majority of these young colonies die or are destroyed within the first 15 months. Before leaving the parent colony each gyne secures a sample of the fungal mycelium in the infrabuccal pocket situated in the jaw. After excavating the first tunnel and brood chamber, the sample of mycelium is regurgitated from the jaw and the female now uses this tiny growth of fungus to establish her new culture. The fungus spreads on to the faeces produced by the female and in turn she eats some of her own eggs for sustenance and also reclaims energy from her now obsolete wing muscles. It is 80 to 100 days before the first worker ants appear but once a certain momentum is reached, at about one year, the growth of the colony is rapid, with nests attaining sizes that vary with each species.

The myrmicine ants have an extensive distribution in South America ranging from approximately 40° latitude north to 44°

Thorns are about all that is left after the workers have finished.

south. *Atta*, the most important species, is confined to a smaller range within the above. The ants have long been, and still are, both revered and feared, mainly due to their tremendously destructive power when encroaching on areas cultivated by man. Almost as soon as the Spanish Conquistadors arrived in the New World, they made note of the depredations of ants, probably *Acromyrmex* or *Atta*. Bartolome De Las Cassas in 1559 described the failure of the Spaniards in Hispaniola to grow cassava and citrus trees because of ants whose nests at the bases of the trees were 'white as snow' (probably the fungus gardens). Article 19 of the Cedula proclaimed by the King of Spain for opening Trinidad to immigration in 1783 stated that 'the Government was to take the utmost care to prevent the introduction of ants into Trinidad'. The ants, of course, had been there all the time.

Of great importance is the impact of leaf cutters on soil nutrition. In tropical rainforest areas few animals and few tree roots go much below the soil surface. In such places a large *Atta* nest contains far more organic matter, in the form of hundreds of fungus gardens, than any other agency in the soil. This organic matter makes possible the multiplication of great quantities of bacteria, nematodes, insects, and other organisms that can only exist deep underground in such numbers because the ants have carried substrate there to give them food and shelter. On the fertile pampas of Argentina the presence of underground nests of *Acromyrmex* is given away by a richer growth of plants above ground.

A nest of *Atta sexdens* was opened up after it has been carefully observed for 47 months. The nest contained 1,027 chambers, of which 390 had active fungus gardens and ants. An enormous chamber was found at a depth of 1.2m (4ft) which was being used as a refuse site and cemetery. The chamber was 90cm (3ft) high and 1.2m (4ft) in diameter. The entomological scientist who removed and noted the contents of this chamber must have been amazed to find that it contained 1,491 adult *Coleoptera*, 15 adult *Diptera*, 56 *Hemiptera*, 40 *Mollusca*, 4 *Reptilia* and one *Pseudo-scorpion*.

There is much more data available that is of tremendous interest. Several modern scientists have spent the whole of their working lives studying the Attini. In such a brief account, I can make scant mention of the four casts, different sized ants within the colonies that have different jobs to do; huge soldiers that protect the nests of *Atta* species, with jaws that can cut another ant in half with one snip or draw blood from a finger without even trying. There are tiny ants which rarely, if ever, venture from the fungus gardens, spending their whole lives tending the fungus and feeding the queen and the ant brood. All the ants have special mouth parts that evolution has adapted to comb the mycelium and remove the gonglylidia when feeding and use a chemical language with dozens of chemicals and compounds.

BREEDING INSTRUCTIONS FOR ACROMYRMEX AND ATTA

It is not difficult to set up a thriving colony of leaf-cutting ants. The most critical factor is temperature. If nest materials are provided together with water the ants will do the rest.

Although they are insects of the tropics, this does not mean they can stand high temperature; this is a grave mistake made by many would-be ant exhibitors. The problem is that at some stage between 27°C (80°F) and 38°C (100°F) the single queen will be rendered infertile. As soon as the last larvae in the nest pupate, no work-inducing pheromones are being produced, and the nest soon begins to deteriorate. The ideal temperature for both *Acromyrmex* and *Atta* is 24–27°C (75–80°F). They will not flourish at temperatures much below or above those levels. I have had more personal success with *Acromyrmex*, but only because they are not quite so susceptible if, despite every effort, the temperature gets a little higher than it should.

Looking at the two species logically, *Acromyrmex* should prove to be the exhibitor's choice, because of possible colony size. One could not hope to cope with a full sized *Atta* colony containing 700,000 to 7 million individuals, depending on the species. *Acromyrmex*, with colony sizes of 10,000 to 20,000 should prove more suitable. Having said this, the queen's lifespan points to *Atta*; at 20 years, she is not only the world's longest-living insect, she also lives twice as long as the small *Acromyrmex* queen. Whichever species you choose, once you have come safely through the first year, your efforts will be greatly rewarded.

I can remember the excitement I felt when I dashed up to London to collect my first colony that had been brought by hand from Trinidad. However, I was disappointed when the plastic box containing the tiny colony was finally handed over. The box contained the queen and about a dozen ants, only one of which was of foraging size. The fungus garden was not of good colour; it should be a light greyish white, but was a dull brown, and only about the size of a walnut.

I had prepared a wooden box 15 × 25cm and 20cm high (6 × 10 × 8in). The side of the box was hinged and made of perspex for viewing the nest. The box contained a small roll of 12mm (½in) mesh chicken wire that just fitted the interior of the box and the whole inner cavity was full of damp soil. A small hole was cut at the base of one end to allow the ants to move in and out; the whole container was placed on a flat stand with a large central leg standing in a tray filled with water to confine the ants to their platform.

I carefully lifted the flap on the side of the box and emptied the contents into a small cavity in the soil. Within minutes, the ants moved the queen out of sight into the soil, and I left them to settle in.

The following day I was delighted to find a considerable amount of soil had been excavated from the box, and almost as soon as I arrived, as if on cue, the one foraging ant made its way from the nest box entrance to the small piece of privet I had placed on the stand in a very shallow container of water; it proceeded to cut a piece of leaf and carry it back to the nest box where it promptly disappeared into the soil. That was in 1974 in late August, and was the first time I had ever seen a leaf-cutting ant cut and carry its tiny parasol. The species was *Acromyrmex octospinosus* and I was also lucky enough to acquire a tiny *Atta cephalotes* colony. The *Atta* colony took off like a rocket, producing visible fungus garden within weeks, but it was nearly three months before a second, very pale looking *Acromyrmex* came out with that lone worker that had arrived with the colony. However, it was the *Acromyrmex* colony that proved to be most successful.

In the following spring the *Atta* colony had grown quite considerably and I was congratulating myself on how well it had done. By that time the *Acromyrmex* had grown to about 100 cutters, and a small garden was visible in their container. We had the first really hot day of spring and I was not on the premises. I arrived at about midday to find the temperature in the ants' quarters around 35°C (in the mid–90's F). Though I cooled it down quickly, the *Atta* colony never recovered and finally faded out. Not being able to bear its last pitiful death throes, I exterminated the last few ants and gave the *Acromyrmex* colony (which recovered well), the last section of *Atta* fungus garden, which they carried into their nest.

The *Acromyrmex* colony went from strength to strength and, at its peak around five years later, six huge fungus gardens, four of which were housed in perspex aquaria 30 × 20 × 20cm (12 × 8 × 8in) were in full operation. I was cramming huge quantities of privet, rose, sycamore, cabbage, Indian bean and orange peel fresh every day. On occasions I also gave them whole apples cut into quarters; they would take four apples in the space of 24 hours.

Dr D. J. Stradling of Exeter University, who had supplied the ants to me, visited the Cotswold Wild Life Park where the ants were on display. He said that he had never seen, even in the wild, such a large colony of *Acromyrmex* and asked me if I had done anything unusual. Using his knowledgeable and clear scientific mind, his questioning finally brought out of me the fact that I had given the ants the fungus from the last garden of my *Atta* colony; this, of course, was why they had done so well. The *Atta* fungus was many times more productive of the gongylidia biomass than the fungus of *Acromyrmex* and so my colony had had the benefit of fungus they would not normally come into contact with. The results of obtaining the *Atta* fungus had made my colony about twice its normal size, probably containing about 30,000 ants at its peak. That colony lasted 11 years, a long life for an *Acromyrmex* queen, and it was my most successful colony.

Throughout its life it was given a new nesting box as soon as it had filled the previous one. Each box was filled with damp soil containing a roll of half inch mesh chicken wire 12mm (½in) to support the gardens as they grew; the soil was thrown out to make room. The display measured 3m (10ft) long, 1.5m (5ft) high and 50cm (20in) deep. Because of the positioning of the tubular heaters, I could only get four aquaria, one on top of the other, to house the fungus gardens. When they were full the ants built fungus garden on the base of the display tank, wherever they could find room; it was a truly wonderful display, discussed and enjoyed by thousands of visitors to the Park, and sadly missed when it finally failed. Looking back on that wonderful display, and with the knowledge I have learned from it, I am at this time negotiating the construction of the most advanced ant display ever seen. This ambitious project will display several large colonies of both *Acromyrmex* and *Atta* working simultaneously in one display unit.

So what do you need to facilitate the successful culture of leaf-cutting ants? You supply the ants with fresh leaves daily, fresh water daily, nest boxes as previously described, the correct temperature (I have always used tubular greenhouse heaters of 60 watts per 30cm (1ft) on a thermostat set at 25°C (77°F).) Supply the ants with all these things and they will do the rest. Always make sure the ants have fresh water and always give them plenty of leaf to last a full 24-hour period. Whether they have used it all or not, replace the leaf supply daily and give them a different leaf every day. Once you have found their favourite leaves, rotate the species so that the ants get variety. At least once a week give them orange peel with leaf and once a week give them a sweet eating apple with leaf.

GUIDE TO FURTHER READING

There are many books on butterflies but the following are a good starting point for delving more deeply into their biology:

D'Abrera, B. (1971–87), *Butterflies of the World: Australian Region, Afro-tropical Region, Neotropical Region Vols. 1, 2 and 3, Oriental Region Vols. 1, 2 and 3,* Lansdowne, Lansdowne & Classey, Hill House, Melbourne.

Ford, E. B. (1957), *Butterflies*, Collins, London.

Lewis, H. L. (1973), *Butterflies of the World*, Albertelli-Leventhal, London.

Owen, D. F. (1971), *Tropical Butterflies*, Oxford University Press, London.

Sbordoni, V. and Forestiero, S. (1985), *The World of Butterflies*, Blandford Press, London.

Scott, J. A. (1985), *The Butterflies of North America*, Standford University, Palo Alto.

Vane-Wright, R. I. and Ackery, P. R. ed. (1984), *The Biology of Butterflies*, Symposium of the Royal Entomological Society of London, Number 11, Academic Press, Inc. (London) Ltd., London. US Edition published by Academic Press (Harcourt Brace Jovanovich, Inc.), Orlando, Florida 32887.

INDEX OF COMMON NAMES

191

INDEX OF SCIENTIFIC NAMES